Living
Justice

Co m e & S e e S e r i e s

The **Come & See Series** from Sheed & Ward is modeled on Jesus' compassionate question: "What do you seek?" and his profound invitation to "Come and see" the world through the eyes of faith (John 1:38–39). The series offers spiritual seekers lively, thought-provoking, and accessible books that explore topics of faith and the Catholic Christian tradition. Each book in the series is written by trustworthy guides who are the very best teachers, theologians, and scholars.

Series Editors: James Martin, S.J.
Jeremy Langford

Living
Justice

Catholic Social Teaching in Action

Thomas Massaro, S.J.

SHEED & WARD

Lanham, Chicago, New York, Oxford

A SHEED & WARD BOOK

ROWMAN & LITTLEFIELD PUBLISHERS, INC.

Published in the United States of America
by Rowman & Littlefield Publishers, Inc.
A wholly owned subsidiary of The Rowman & Littlefield Publishing Group, Inc.
4501 Forbes Boulevard, Suite 200, Lanham, Maryland 20706
www.rowmanlittlefield.com

PO Box 317, Oxford, OX2 9RU, UK

Printed in the United States of America

Cover and interior design: Biner Design and GrafixStudio, Inc.

Cover art: "The Banquet" by Ansgar Holmberg, CSJ, St. Paul, Minnesota

Library of Congress Cataloging-in-Publication Data

Massaro, Thomas, 1961–
    Living justice : Catholic social teaching in action / Thomas Massaro
        p. cm. — (Come & see series)
    Includes bibliographical references and index.
    ISBN 1-58051-046-9 (alk. paper)
        1. Sociology, Christian (Catholic) 2. Church and social
        problems—Catholic Church. 3. Catholic Church—Doctrines.
        I. Title. II. Come & see
BX1753 .M354 2000
261.8'088'22—dc21   00-024788
                                                           CIP

Contents

Preface

This book is intended as an introduction to the tradition of social ethics within the Roman Catholic Church. It assumes no previous knowledge of the subject and defines any technical terms when they first appear. I hope that the style and choice of topics will invite into the conversation many people who have never read anything about Catholic teachings on justice, peace, and other social issues.

Sometimes when I introduce myself as a seminary professor who specializes in Catholic social teaching, people ask me what they can read as a first step to understanding this important field. My inability up until now to answer this question prompted me to write this book. While many people, both inside and outside the Church, have heard of Catholic social teaching, there has never been a single volume that answers the most obvious questions that arise in the minds of nonexperts.

Because this work cannot anticipate every question that might come up, "For Further Study" (page 241) lists resources for additional information on the topics covered in that chapter. One great way to use this book is to share your reactions to each chapter with a small group of friends. The "Questions for Reflection" that accompany each chapter provide you with good starting points for these conversations.

Some readers might find it helpful to skip around, reading the chapters in a different order than they appear. The first two chapters answer the broad questions that might arise about why and how any church or religious group might speak about public issues that we usually think of as political or economic in nature. Chapter three traces the history of Catholic social teaching and highlights the concerns for justice in the modern world that led bishops and popes to write documents addressing the world beyond the doors of the Church. Chapter four looks at Scripture, natural law, social analysis, and other theological traditions that contribute to the style and substance of Catholic social teaching. The nine most important themes of that teaching are treated in chapter five. Chapter six contrasts the viewpoint of Catholic social teaching with communism and libertarian capitalism–two ideological systems that Catholic social teaching has critiqued for many decades. The final chapter looks to the future and contains my predictions for themes, old and new, that might play a major role in our new millennium as the Church continues to address political, social, and economic issues.

The great thing about studying social justice, unlike some other topics in theology, is that everyone has opinions and probably some experience. Even if you do not agree with all of my opinions and approaches, I encourage you to reflect on your own personal experience to make informed judgments about goals and strategies for the improvement of society.

I wish to thank all the people who, over many years, have helped me understand and develop the ideas in this book: the many teachers, classmates, and students who took the time to debate with me the merits of various views of justice. I am especially indebted to Jim Martin, S.J. and Mark Kolakowski, who read early versions of each chapter.

I dedicate this book to my parents, Joseph and Nancy Massaro, who were my first teachers in the ways of justice, fairness, and concern for all people. They have joined their efforts to those of a multitude of believers, both laity and clergy, to practice, promote, and teach justice in a world so desperately in need of faith, hope, and love. As is written in the Book of Daniel, "Those who lead the many to justice shall be like the stars forever" (Daniel 12:3).

Chapter 1

An Invitation to Catholic Social Ethics

Consider these situations you might observe on any given day:

A twelve-year-old boy saves his allowance for over a month to buy the newly released CD from his favorite rap band. After making his purchase, and with less than a dollar left in change, he steps outside the sleek revolving door of the music store thinking about the candy bar he will purchase and enjoy on the walk home. Just at that moment he notices a street person leaning against a nearby lamppost and cradling a crude cardboard sign that reads: "WILL WORK FOR FOOD." He must have passed this man on the way into the store but, in anticipation of spending his hard-earned money, he didn't notice. Now, as the boy takes a closer look, he notices that the man resembles his own grandfather—the same uneven stubble on his face, similar crows feet above either cheek, the same type of suspenders—but with a far more weary look in his hollow eyes. The boy empties his pocket change into the old fellow's rough palm and scampers down the street at a bit faster pace than usual.

∽

A young lawyer, straight out of law school, hears about the huge backlog of cases in the Immigration and Naturalization Service system. It disturbs her that refugees and immigrants seeking U.S. residency because of fear of political persecution in their homelands must wait many months in federal detention centers before they secure the legal assistance and court time to have their requests for asylum status heard. After some reflection, the young woman decides to squeeze into her busy schedule at least ten hours a month to volunteer her legal services as an advocate for a few of these detainees on a *pro bono* basis.

∽

An aging couple have joked for years about looking forward to experiencing "empty-nest syndrome" once the last of their four children leaves home for college. Now that this has finally happened, they have started to plan weekend getaways and long trips that they have been delaying for years. Then they read a newspaper article about their state's desperate shortage of foster homes, where orphans or children from troubled families might receive temporary care in a domestic setting with more warmth and comfort than other institutional options. The couple considers many facets of their situation: their three empty bedrooms, the sacrifice of freedom and mobility that would accompany this new commitment, the risk that some of the kids they host might become violent or bring drugs into their home. In the end, they decide to complete an application to become foster parents.

Each of these stories is about an ordinary decision made by ordinary people. The boy, the young lawyer, and the aging couple are not likely to think of themselves as involved in the cause of social justice, but their acts of generosity, however small, amount to a real contribution to building a better society.

Every year thousands of people make many different kinds of commitments to the advancement of social justice. They might volunteer on a weekly or monthly basis to help provide social services at a local community center, work at a soup kitchen or homeless shelter, assist through clerical support at a drug-counseling program, answer phones at a crisis hotline, or offer their E.M.T. skills at a local volunteer fire department. They might use a portion of their inherited or earned wealth to establish a charitable trust or foundation to alleviate poverty.

People who have less to give might resolve to make a conscious effort to respond more often and more generously to those heart-rending letters from charitable organizations. They might choose to go beyond financial assistance and part-time volunteering to make a deeper commitment, perhaps giving a year or more of their lives to service work for and with the least fortunate members of society, whether in their homeland or overseas. Others deliberately accept lower-paying careers with a service dimension because they want to make a positive difference in the lives of others—at least a few. Nobody gets rich working in inner-city schools or doing community organizing, but this kind of work attracts an often surprising number of talented people.

It is safe to say that the decisions of these generous people would receive applause from just about any audience; it simply warms our hearts to learn of selfless efforts that benefit the least fortunate members of society. We can all agree that the world would be a better place if more of us more often made decisions like those described above. Nobody wants the problems of poverty, homelessness, inadequate health care, and legal assistance for vulnerable populations to continue unchecked or worsen in the future. To be human is to have a heart that is moved by stories of desperate need and crying injustices. Humanitarian responses to people in crisis are practically instinctual.

Why Make an Effort for Social Justice? The Religious Motivation

While all of us would like to see less suffering and more social justice in the world, an interesting question is: Why do some people choose to get involved while others do not? What ideas or motivations impel certain members of society to make significant sacrifices of their time, energy, and money to help others? What gives some people the energy and loving-kindness to perform generous actions and undertake altruistic projects that most people approve of but fail to tackle themselves? While all of us have the frequent experience of "our hearts going out to the needy," why is it that some of us "reach out" to our neighbors in need while some of us don't?

There are many secular-minded humanitarians in our midst who are motivated by genuine concern for other people. These people may explain their compassionate response to suffering and injustice in terms of a desire to assist the project of human development, the cause of human rights, or the well-being of a specific nation, region, city, or ethnic group. They may gladly line up under any number of banners, such as "secular humanism," the "human rights movement," "feminism," "Black Power," or even "universal solidarity." Some of these people resist all attempts to label the sources of their social concerns, preferring to steer clear of being identified with any specific cause, ideology, or philosophy. They may be satisfied with the simple explanation that their work for justice is merely a response to a personal inner calling they feel to "give something back" and "do one's duty to others."

Many people, however, are eager to identify their charitable works with their religious beliefs. They are quite articulate about why they perform philanthropic activities: to do the will of God in the world, to promote the sacred dignity of the lives of their neighbors in need, to spread the gospel in a concrete way, to reflect the love of God to others, to be a witness to Jesus Christ and the Kingdom of God while here on earth. Religiously motivated people sometimes direct their energies toward church-based activities and work with agencies and programs that are obviously religious, such as

Catholic Charities, the Saint Vincent de Paul Society, Pax Christi, Covenant House, or the Salvation Army. At other times, similar efforts may be motivated by religiously inspired ideas but do not proceed under the auspices of any church or religious institution.

When religious people who are engaged in the work of social justice talk about what motivates their activities, they usually connect these acts of "love of neighbor" with the "love of God," which is at the root of the life of faith. As Dorothy Day, the founder of the Catholic Worker, says on the final page of her autobiography, *The Long Loneliness*, "We cannot love God unless we love each other." These words echo several sayings of Jesus, who closely unites our response to the needs of our neighbor to our relationship with God, a relationship that supports and justifies all we do on earth.

This connection between heavenly and earthly realities is tricky business. Recognizing within ourselves a desire to respond to God's call for us to build a more just world is only the beginning of a long journey of discernment. How will we know which actions are authentic responses to God's love? How do we choose between alternate ways of donating our time, money, and energy in good works? Should we give priority to responding to the immediate needs of the least advantaged, or is it better to focus on long-range solutions that cannot be accused of functioning as mere "band-aids"?

How widely should we cast our net of concern? These are difficult questions. The good news is that we are not alone in our attempts to answer them.

In a sense, we are standing on the shoulders of giants, where we can take advantage of many traditions of reflection on these perennial questions. In fact, every religion and every secular ideology has an implicit or explicit way of addressing these questions. There are well-formulated sets of answers for Marxists, utilitarians, libertarians, Hindus, Jews, Muslims, Mennonites, and Lutherans. This book will focus on just one tradition: Roman Catholicism. Over the past century, the Catholic Church has developed a body of social teachings that has grown increasingly insightful, challenging, and sophisticated in helping us shape our personal and collective responses to social concerns such as poverty and injustice.

The subsequent chapters of this book explore the intellectual resources of Catholic social teaching: what it says, why it makes these claims, and how we can apply these insights in our everyday lives. Even if studying the message of Catholic social thought will not dramatically change what you are doing in the name of social justice, it will at least deepen your reflections on the "why" questions. Familiarity with the ethical stances articulated by popes and bishops may allow you to get a better grip on your own motivations and strategies for engaging in social activism and charitable work.

The story of the Church's involvement in social justice is a story of growth, much as a small seed sprouts from its modest beginnings to become a living and full-flowering organism. Over the past few generations, Catholic clergy and laity have been growing in the direction of a more socially responsible stance toward political and economic issues that affect the lives of all people. It is reassuring to note that we are not alone in this regard. There is a remarkable convergence among people of many different faiths in religious communities that have been walking along parallel paths in recent years. With regard to concern about promoting justice and the content of their justice message, religious voices from very diverse traditions have been echoing one another in recent decades, calling for many of the same reforms and advocating many of the same measures.

Ecumenical and interreligious agreement and collaboration in the area of justice has become so strong and obvious that a revealing slogan has been coined: "Where doctrine divides, the practice of pursuing social justice unites." Even while the world's many religions remain at odds on theological questions, religious approaches to social justice have a way of bringing all of us together. This is especially obvious when it comes time to stop theorizing about what should be done and to get down to rolling up our sleeves and engaging in serious work for service and social change.

Still, differences remain among the approaches of members of different religions, including the various branches of Christianity. It is indeed comforting to find overlapping messages on social justice from religions leaders, but it would be foolish to claim that these leaders are in complete agreement about everything. Even when we agree that some things are wrong, that lamentable situations of injustice exist in our world, there are a variety of possible responses. Some people, for example, are inclined to be passive, resigning themselves to the *status quo*, at least for the time being. To justify their stance, they may cite core beliefs about "God's providence" or their confidence in eventual vindication.

Others become extremely impatient and can imagine no constructive course of action except immediate (and perhaps violent) revolution, advocating a sharp break from current ways of doing "business as usual." The vast majority, however, find themselves somewhere between these two extremes. As these people try to cling to what is helpful in the present socioeconomic system, even while working for gradual improvement, they make use of whatever sources of inspiration and explanation they can find in traditions of thought about social order. They find inspiration in the words and actions of those who have gone before them seeking to discover the way of justice and social responsibility. It is especially for these that this book about Catholic social teaching is written.

Social Mission and Church Morale

It is no secret that many adult Catholics feel somewhat alienated from the Church. For a variety of reasons, and against the backdrop of often painful personal experiences, millions of Catholics harbor some degree of doubt about their attachment to their parish, their diocese, perhaps even the entire structure of Roman Catholicism. They may experience diminishing enthusiasm for attending parish activities, perhaps even staying away from liturgy and worship. Entire families sometimes waver in their practice of the faith, some even to the point of no longer identifying themselves as Catholics.

The causes of this malaise are complex and no doubt vary from person to person and place to place. Some people may be impatient or distressed by a seeming preoccupation of church authorities with the orthodoxy of certain liberal theologians. Endless debates over the fine points of arcane doctrine and the exercise of ecclesiastical discipline seem irrelevant to these people, especially when their hunger for deeper union with God is not being fed by the sermons they hear Sunday after Sunday and the various programs that are supposed to nourish parish life. Many thoughtful Catholics find themselves depressed and exhausted by frequent conversations about the declining number of priests and nuns, the future of parish life, inclusive language in the liturgy, the necessity of an all-male and all-celibate priesthood, and ecclesiastical politics in general.

The mere act of turning to the topic of Catholic social teaching, of course, does not automatically solve the problem of declining church morale. It certainly does not settle all the debates over church practices and policies, each of which demands serious attention in every locality. But there is an immense benefit in refocusing our energies as a church to the world beyond our front doors—to the struggle for social justice that affects people around the world, not just a limited circle or a few elites. Becoming more aware of the great issues of our day—from hunger to the plight of refugees to environmental crises to the cessation of war—has a way of putting into perspective the squabbles that take place within the walls of the Church. Many Catholics who found their energies for church life flagging have received great encouragement from learning more about the Church's principled and often courageous stances on peace, justice, and human rights.

Catholic social teaching can serve as a unifying force, a banner under which believers may rally even if they remain somewhat divided on certain matters about the internal life of the Church. Even allowing for some differences of opinion between liberals and conservatives over how to apply the message of Catholic social teaching to concrete problems, we can look to the Church's teaching on economic, political, and social issues with pride and hope.

Sharing "Our Best Kept Secret"

When outsiders think of the Roman Catholic Church, many images and ideas surely come to mind. For example, they may identify our Church with the face of a prominent pope, cardinal, or bishop, or they may recall the sweet smell of incense, the beauty of a stained glass window, or the soothing melody of Gregorian chant. It is unlikely, however, that many would make such a quick association between Catholicism and the notion of social justice. For this reason, Catholic social teaching has often been called "our best kept secret." In fact, some people are astonished when they first hear of the Church's commitment to justice throughout the world. How can an institution like the Catholic Church, long associated with a "conservative" approach that resists change and looks to the past, have been delivering for so long a progressive message that challenges the global economic and political order? Part of the mission of Catholics today is to expose this "secret" and share the riches of this tradition with the wider community of concerned people.

The sharing of this secret has already started in ways that may not be obvious. In fact, many of the laudable social institutions and practices that we take for granted today have their roots in teachings and activities of the Christian community, including the Catholic Church. For example, the complex system of hospitals and modern health care from which we all benefit sprang from charitable works that were sponsored by churches, both Protestant and Catholic, in previous centuries. Modern labor unions and group insurance policies are an outgrowth of various activities of guilds and sodalities, agencies through which members of the medieval Church practiced mutual support, often under direct religious auspices. Churches organized the first schools in our nation and in other lands, and much of our educational system at all levels is still religiously affiliated. It was the Church that cared for poor families before there were public social service agencies. The contemporary social work and nursing professions grew out of the efforts of church personnel, largely nuns and laywomen, Catholic and Protestant alike, to assist families in need of resources, expertise, and healing.

For good reason, then, the Church has been called the "godmother of the nonprofit sector." The Church continues to have significant impact on the shape of all these activities and professions as well as various social movements for justice, civil rights, and a more humane world. In fact, there is a recurring historical pattern by which assorted efforts begin with religious motivations and zeal, and then come to be regularized and routinized in the form of secular institutions. This is a beneficial, constructive aspect of the Church's service to the world and in no way diminishes the Church, as long as we remain conscious of the way these developments are a credit to the Church and its efforts at advancing social justice in our world.

From "Charity Alone" to a Justice Orientation

Over the past few decades, the Church has witnessed a significant shift in how it understands its mission to contribute to the fight against poverty. To illustrate this point, compare the Catholic Church of the nineteenth century to the same Church of today. In the United States and Europe, the work of the Church in the earlier era emphasized the role of charitable efforts as being the key to its social mission. In those years, the Church attempted primarily to inspire good works among its members, especially those with the means to assist their less fortunate neighbors. According to that approach, charity was an unsystematic, episodic, and largely personal issue. The most church officials felt they could do was to appeal to the private consciences of individuals and perhaps "fill in the cracks" by sending missionaries and members of religious orders to attempt to meet some of the more desperate needs that were not being met through the generosity of anyone else. The heroic effort on the part of many groups of religious sisters in this era are especially to be commended. These women religious selflessly founded and staffed orphanages, schools for the children of immigrants, and various charitable agencies that supplied food, clothing, housing, and other forms of assistance to millions.

The Church of today continues to do many of these same good works, but it supplements its *charitable* efforts with efforts that contribute to the promotion of *justice.* The contemporary Church speaks about issues and undertakes efforts that were unheard of a century ago. The National Conference of Catholic Bishops in Washington, D.C., for example, includes an office dedicated to lobbying members of Congress and the executive branch of government. The purpose of these lobbying efforts on the part of the Bishops' Conference is not to win special favors for the Church, as if Catholic religious leaders were just another special interest pushing a selfish agenda. Rather, the goal is to persuade influential government officials to enact programs that will advance the causes of peace, public morality, and social justice.

By maintaining a presence on Capitol Hill, the American Catholic bishops seek to serve as advocates for the less privileged members of society—low-income families, the homeless, recent immigrants. These are the same demographic groups that, in previous eras and according to the older model of *charity alone*, the Church assisted primarily through direct relief, as the conduit of donations of money, goods, and services. The difference is that today, according to the newer model of church activity that emphasizes *justice in addition to charity*, more church efforts are indirect attempts to change social structures (including civil laws and government budget priorities) so that all people may have a better and fairer chance of living a good life.

Church lobbying to advocate fairer laws may seem like a controversial and indirect way to advance social justice. But a more direct and less contested set of efforts is organized under the auspices of the Catholic Campaign for Human Development (CCHD). Since 1969, this organization has been funded and overseen by the U.S. Catholic bishops. The CCHD is dedicated to education and self-help programs designed to support the achievement of greater social justice in localities around the country. The overarching goal is to empower all people to participate fully in the life of our society so that no one is deprived of the freedom and rights we take for granted. Every year, the CCHD assists projects such as rural cooperatives in Appalachia, adult education programs for migrant farm workers, and community-based micro-enterprise projects that provide jobs in inner cities, on Indian reservations, and in areas suffering from high unemployment.

From its beginning, the CCHD has been a source of hope for those who often seem forgotten. Some impressive victories against injustice and inequality have been achieved by encouraging people to work together on the local level. Catholics can be proud that their Church provides the financial and logistical resources to empower people to improve their lives through building up the local community and breaking the cycle of poverty and dependence.

Besides lobbying and the CCHD, there are other examples that illustrate how the Church's response to poverty and injustice has shifted in recent decades. There are certainly many *continuities* with the past, such as the Church's constant concern for the well-being of the least advantaged, its call for personal conversion toward care for others, and the willingness to perform direct service to the poor in moments of crisis or dire need. But there are also striking elements of *change*. For example, we now enjoy an expanded view of what is needed to foster total human development. As a result, we are committed to creating a social as well as a physical environment that is healthy for humanity. We now have a broader sense of what efforts are appropriate for the Church to undertake in its mission of service to the gospel and the world.

To our existing belief in the benefits of charity, we have added a commitment to justice. Where *charity* tends to involve individuals or small groups of people acting to meet the immediate needs of others, work for *justice* involves a more communal and even global awareness of problems and their potential long-term solutions. Where the notion of *charity* calls to mind voluntary giving out of one's surplus, the notion of *justice* suggests that there is an absolute obligation to share the benefits of God's creation more broadly than we see in the present order.

Because justice makes demands upon us to practice social responsibility, we cannot ignore its call to work through large institutions, including government, to change the structures that perpetuate poverty and keep the least powerful members of society from achieving their human potential. That the Church has begun to reflect on the underlying structures that breed injustice, to speak of the demands of justice, and to advocate changes on the local, national, and international level is indeed a great advancement. The Church's commitment to structural change is a relatively new face of her awareness of her social mission.

This does not mean that the Church has somehow abandoned the way of charity or hands-on neighbor-to-neighbor assistance; by no means has the Church announced that love comes up short. Rather, we have discovered a unity between love and justice. In a world that has grown increasingly complex, we have found that love travels best through well-worn routes we call *structures* and *institutions*. The Church is finding itself increasingly aware of how the well-being of the most vulnerable depends upon the fairness of these structures and institutions, and has bravely committed itself in recent decades to the transformation of the world for the welfare of all God's children. As it often does, the Church is offering a "both/and" solution to what is often portrayed as an "either/or" option. In other words, we need not choose between justice and charity. Rather, we can seek the best way to combine heroic acts of love with a clearheaded view of the importance of justice that must be regularized and routinized in fair institutions that respond to the needs and dignity of all.

Let us not delude ourselves, however, by taking on an exaggerated sense of the importance of any human efforts for justice. No matter how well the Church fulfills her mission to justice, the imperfect conditions of this sinful world will always leave us falling short of the righteous order that we call God's kingdom. No amount of effort on the part of humans will ever transform social conditions into a utopia or paradise.

The ultimate basis for our hopes is always bound up with God and can never rest solely on human efforts. At the same time, of course, we must not overlook the importance of continued fidelity to the Church's mission to do justice. As the 1971 Synod of Catholic Bishops in Rome boldly declared:

> Action on behalf of justice and participation in the transformation of the world fully appear to us as a constitutive dimension of the preaching of the Gospel, or, in other words, of the Christian mission for the redemption of the human race and its liberation from every oppressive situation (no. 6).

Looking Ahead

In this chapter we have explored the importance of Catholic social teaching in the life of the Church. The remainder of this book attempts to explain what the Church says about the social, political, and economic realities of our world. Chapter two describes the major features of the dialogue between the Church and the world, between the life of faith and the public life of a nation. Chapter three investigates the history of

Catholic social teaching and explores some of the historical forces that shaped its development. Chapter four describes the sources and methods of Catholic social thought, presenting a simple picture of where it gets its principles and how it makes its judgments about the contemporary world. Chapter five examines in greater detail the content and central themes of this message that the Church brings to the world. Chapter six brings Catholic social teaching into dialogue with other common schools of thought that serve as its rivals and critics. Finally, chapter seven closes our study by speculating about future directions and priorities that might emerge in Catholic social teaching.

Questions for Reflection

1. Do you know anyone who participates in philanthropic activities without any underlying religious motivations? How would you characterize their motivations?

2. Which parts of the Bible, or which figures in Christian history, seem to inspire the Church in its mission to justice? How would your answer be different if the question ended with the phrase "its mission to charity"?

3. What factors contribute to the low profile of Catholic social teaching? Would the Church be much different if it were not "our best kept secret"?

4. Does the shift in church social action from a model of *charity* to a *justice* orientation make you uncomfortable? What are the dangers and how can the Church avoid them?

Chapter 2

Going Public with Your Faith

Most children learn at an early age that some topics are suitable for public conversations and others are to be kept strictly private. It would be a matter of bad manners and a source of potentially great embarrassment, for example, to reveal to a wide audience the details of what goes on in the private recesses of a household. Although outsiders may be amused when "kids say the darnedest things," nobody denies that certain topics (such as which chemicals we use on our graying hair and which bedclothes we choose to wear or not wear!) should remain off limits in public conversations.

Where should we draw these lines? Is the subject of our life of faith something to be kept private? Recall the old saying that there are two subjects that should never be broached in polite conversation: religion and politics. This chapter challenges the wisdom of that adage. It suggests that a mature and socially responsible faith will insist that we not only talk about both topics, but must not shy away from the controversial task of addressing religion and politics together.

Building a Bridge between Two Worlds

Talking about religious and political matters in the same breath makes most people a bit nervous; we are much more comfortable when we find a way to segregate these two topics into separate compartments. The modern world has by and large benefited from the process by which religious matters are differentiated from political affairs. Perhaps as far back as prehistoric times, people began to appoint religious leaders—often called "priests," "shamans," or "holy" men or women—who were distinct from their chieftain, king, queen, or village leader.

For many reasons, this division between religious and political office makes good sense; it allows both fields to benefit from the specialized knowledge of those who concentrate on one human endeavor. The skills required to lead us in prayer or to console us in time of mourning, for example, do not readily translate into the world of treaty negotiation, law enforcement, or public finance. Setting up clear lines of demarcation allows both religious and political leaders to fulfill appropriate roles and carve out proper spheres of legitimate authority. Only the foolish person would claim competence in all arenas, and only a foolish society would entrust one person with the full range of both political and religious duties.

But this separation of functions is not the final word on the relationship between our spiritual and our political lives. Just as mayors sometimes need to consult with priests and prophets seek to bend the ears of kings, dialogue between the spiritual and the temporal worlds benefits each sphere and is necessary for the well-being of both church and state. On some issues, we find that concerns of secular and religious leaders converge and overlap, as the borders between the two blur. Matters of public policy invariably contain moral dimensions in which religious leaders have a stake. On the other hand, religious organizations like churches find themselves involved in activities with political implications and in which public officials have a stake. Thus, the way we organize our political lives is never completely sealed off from our deepest spiritual values and our picture of ultimate cosmic truths.

The interplay of religion and politics has been a constant concern of Christianity throughout its history. Jesus addresses the issue in oblique ways when he claims that his kingdom is not of this world (see John 18:36) but, at the same time, his followers are to "repay to Caesar what belongs to Caesar and to God what belongs to God" (Luke 20:20–26). Saint Paul recommends that we adopt a stance of obedience to civil authorities (see Romans 13:1–7), but elsewhere in the New Testament (see Revelation 13:1–10) government is portrayed as demonic in nature—at the very least not to be distrusted and perhaps even to be resisted.

The early centuries of Christianity found the members of Christian communities attempting to live within a Roman Empire they at once admired and feared. Government certainly had the power to persecute them in the most violent ways, and it did so sporadically. Yet the early Christians were also aware that government could be a force for immense good in the world. After the conversion of Emperor Constantine early in the fourth century and the eventual establishment of Christianity as the official religion of the empire, for example, popes, bishops, priests, and lay Christians forged a rather cozy (some say too cozy) relationship with government officials, even to the point of using the structures of the Roman Empire to spread Christian belief to new corners of the world.

Tertullian's Question

Amidst some years of uneasy relations between Church and empire, a North African Christian named Tertullian asked a simple but provocative question: "What has Jerusalem to say to Athens?" His inquiry was not really a matter of geography, for he was speaking metaphorically. The Greek city of Athens represented all the treasures of secular culture, including the great traditions of learning and the arts that came from pagan figures such as Homer, Sophocles, Plato, and Aristotle. Jerusalem, capital of the Holy Land, sacred to the Jewish tradition and the city whose streets Jesus had trod, stood for the heritage of biblical faith and religious piety. At the start of the third century, Tertullian's reflections were suggesting questions we still wrestle with today: How can and should we relate our citizenship and discipleship? How can we simultaneously remain participants in the life of the *Church* and participants in a *secular culture* that resists and even rejects the demands of faith?

Tertullian's question opens a debate about the relationship between faith and culture, between church and world, between the demands of our religion and our participation in political life. It asks us to take an inventory of our deepest loyalties as citizens and as Christians. Do we identify more with our secular culture or with our religious commitments? To what extent is it necessary to make a choice between these two aspects of our lives?

When people consider Tertullian's question and survey their own reactions, two patterns of response tend to emerge. On the one hand, there are those who emphasize the possibilities for harmonious fusion between faith and culture, between the gospel and the world as we know it. Call this the "both/and" option. A person of sincere Christian faith, it seems to these people, can function quite well in the public world marked as it is by pluralism and a great variety of value systems. Religious people can blend right in with others without undue tension or discomfort. In public life, there is no reason why we cannot readily make common cause with non-Christians, for our values are not all that different. Dialogue and mutual understanding between gospel and culture, between the Church and the secular state, are possible and indeed promising endeavors.

The other set of potential answers to Tertullian's question belongs to those people who judge modern culture in an entirely different light. They hold the "either/or" type of opinion and are much more pessimistic about the prospects for successfully balancing Christian identity with membership in secular society. They emphasize the inevitability of deep, even radical conflict between the two. This stance is sometimes referred to as the "sectarian option" and includes a hostility on the part of some people of faith to nonreligious sources of wisdom—a distrust of science, academic philosophy, and the school of social thought called *secular humanism.*

While we must be careful not to exaggerate or caricature this approach to social life, the sectarian option is most evident in the lifestyles of entire communities that attempt to live apart from most modern influences. One familiar example is found in the Amish people of Southeastern Pennsylvania. The "Pennsylvania Dutch," as they are sometimes (quite inaccurately) called, deliberately shun a majority of modern conveniences and technological advances that the rest of us take for granted. They do not make these choices out of an idle romantic nostalgia for the past but as a matter of principle, based on the same beliefs that lead them to avoid as much contact as possible with government, the court system, and the military. Other adherents of sectarianism are prompted by their beliefs to withdraw from the wider society in smaller, less noticeable ways. For example, they may choose

to educate their children privately (home schooling) or boycott elections or the media because they judge the cultural
mainstream to be somehow antithetical to their personal religious values.

Most Catholics today have considerable difficulty
imagining a life of withdrawal from the social mainstream as
practiced by followers of the sectarian option. The dominant
approach within the Catholic Church features an ethic of
social engagement—a willingness to get deeply involved in
society despite an awareness of the flaws and injustices of the
present social order. If social institutions are found to be corrupt, then the proper response is to take on some responsibility for transforming structures and procedures to make
them measure up to reasonable standards. If there is something disturbing about the dominant culture of an age,
Catholics usually do not ask how quickly they can find an exit
route to flee the disaster but, rather, how they can contribute
to changing the objectionable features and practices of society so that it better reflects their religiously grounded values.

According to this ethic of social engagement, the two
most extreme answers to Tertullian's question ("nothing" and
"everything") are both misguided and potentially dangerous.
If we were to claim that "Jerusalem" has *nothing* to say to
"Athens," we would be giving up the struggle before it begins.
It would be irresponsible to deprive society of the contribu-

tion of religiously motivated persons whose ideas and energies are the potential basis for much needed activism and social movements for great improvement. To take just a few examples from our own country, where would American society be if religious groups had not agitated for an end to slavery (in the Abolition movement), to extreme militarism (the peace movement), to racial injustice (the Civil Rights movement), and to extreme poverty (the fight against hunger, homelessness, and illiteracy)?

Each of these movements witnessed the formation of an effective coalition for social change, and religious groups were key partners in all these coalitions. On some occasions, religious leaders even played a dominant role, but they were always willing to make common cause with people motivated by secular reasons for the transformation of society toward greater justice and compassion. Sometimes the rhetoric of the resulting coalition borrowed religious language to advance the cause; words like "covenant" and phrases like the "Good Samaritan" and "my brother's keeper" become rallying points even for atheists working for change. Examples from other cultures and ages would confirm our conclusion that "Jerusalem" clearly has something to offer "Athens."

Just as we should not claim that Jerusalem has nothing to offer Athens, we would also be foolish to suggest that Jerusalem has *everything* to say to Athens. In other words, it would be misguided and even dangerous to claim that religious messages should dictate the terms of public policy or social institutions in a complex, pluralistic society. Even those who look favorably upon the way religious traditions inspire greater morality and justice in society wisely recognize the limits of religious influence on the workings of politics. To forget this insight is to risk sliding into a situation of crass theocracy—literally the "rule of religion" where public policy is at the beck and call of religious leaders. Even assuming that a given society could agree on the matter of precisely which religious leaders speak with the necessary authority to determine social priorities and strategies, there are numerous reasons to avoid this situation.

We have already noted the way this failure to distinguish between religious and political functions deprives society of the benefits of specialization of experts in distinct spheres of activity. Let us examine a second objection to an exaggerated public role for "Jerusalem": the way a theocratic approach misapplies religious zeal and idealism to the political world of realism and compromise.

The Perils of the Crusading Spirit

Religion evokes our deepest aspirations for meaning and proper order in the universe. In the contexts of both our personal lives and our life in society, religious zeal possesses remarkable power to inspires us to make great sacrifices and undertake heroic efforts to achieve laudable goals. Reading stories of the lives of the saints, for example, reminds us of some of the commendable achievements that have been inspired by faith commitments. On this "micro" level of individual lives and face-to-face relations, we easily reach the conclusion that immense good has been done in the name of faith.

History books, on the other hand, give us a more balanced account of the positive and negative influence of religious motivations on the larger, "macro" level of society, especially on political affairs. Every age of human history has witnessed destructive and violent behavior justified by religious reasons. While some of these abuses stemmed from cynical opportunism on the part of religious or political officeholders, others may be attributed to leaders who were quite sincere in their expression of religious motivations but applied religious ideas in inappropriate ways for misguided political agendas.

Perhaps the best examples of religious commitment gone awry are the Crusades. Literally, the word *crusade* refers to "an effort that unfolds under the shadow and protection of the cross" (the Latin word for cross is *crux*, the root word of crusade). The word has come to gather the connotation of any militant struggle undertaken for reasons of religion or deeply held ideological beliefs. In the late medieval world, popes and bishops of Western Christianity preached fervent sermons in an attempt to inspire knights, peasants, and even children to take up arms, make mass pilgrimages to the Holy Land or other regions on the edge of Christendom, and defeat nonbelievers in holy combat. Muslims and Jews were demonized as "infidels" against whom any means of warfare was justified. The authority of God's will, as interpreted by officeholders in the Christian church, was invoked as the wellspring of these repeated efforts to claim sacred places for Christ at the point of a sword.

Other episodes in Christian history display the same logic of limitless violence in service to a divinely sanctioned cause. Most notable among them is the Inquisition, a centuries-long effort to uphold orthodox belief by subjecting suspected heretics to investigation, imprisonment, and even torture if necessary to defend the purity of the faith. Without a doubt, the Inquisition represents one of the darkest chapters in the history of the Catholic Church.

Lest anyone think this perversion of religious motivation is limited to Christianity, however, it is instructive to note how the peculiar notion of "holy war" has been applied throughout history by numerous religious groups, from the Muslim jihad to extreme forms of Jewish Zionism and Hindu separatism in the Indian subcontinent. The only thing these groups have in common is a zealous devotion to a particular notion of divine will and enough power to exert their geopolitical will through force of arms. The core contents of faith that (with rare exceptions) are oriented toward peace, such as love and respect for others, come to be twisted by temptations toward greed, hatred, and distrust of the alien—motives that unleash unspeakable outbursts of violence and terrorism against innocent persons caught in the crossfire. The damage done is multiplied when these misguided religious energies capture the apparatus of government and apply the coercive power of a state for inappropriate ends.

Two instructive episodes in the history of the United States also reflect this dynamic of the misapplication of religious zeal to politics, but on a more limited scale than the medieval Crusades. The first is the growth of the concept of Manifest Destiny, the notion that our nation somehow received a divine mission to spread its territorial control and distinctive way of life from Atlantic to Pacific, to become a continental power under the approving eyes of God. On the surface, this patriotic idea seems acceptable enough until we think back to the geographical realities of the early decades of our new nation, when this ideology was beginning to blossom. The extreme version of Manifest Destiny ignored one key "inconvenient" fact: the land over which we seemed destined to expand was by no means vacant territory. The area that now comprises the western United States was populated by native Americans and residents of Mexico, and both groups had prior claim to the millions of square acres of land our American forebears so coveted.

Although Manifest Destiny was not a formal theological doctrine of any specific Christian denomination, this religiously based ideology helped provoke the Mexican War of 1846–1848 and the numerous violent campaigns that nearly exterminated the tribal peoples we usually call American Indians. Although historians differ in interpreting the significance and degree of culpability for some of these developments, these sad episodes demonstrate that American Christians are by no means immune from the logic of the "crusade." The doctrine of Manifest Destiny that justified U.S. land grabs that expanded our nation was a product of religious zeal that entered the world of politics only to leave destructive and regrettable effects in its wake.

A second example from American history involves much less violence, but it does round out our picture of the problems inherent in bringing a crusading religious spirit into large-scale politics. Near the top of the agenda of many religious leaders in the United States a century ago was the campaign to outlaw the production and consumption of alcoholic beverages. Starting in the nineteenth century, religious forces, especially in conservative Protestant denominations, teamed up with others to form effective coalitions such as the Anti-Saloon League and the Women's Christian Temperance Union. These coalitions, first on the state level and subsequently on the national level, won impressive legal victories to restrict the availability and use of liquor.

To support the cause of temperance, a range of arguments, both theological and practical in nature, were spelled out: the evil effects of intoxication on family life and public morals; the unconscionable waste of valuable grain, time, and money on the production of alcohol, drinking, and associated vices; the corruption of wanton escapism and alcoholic excess prohibited by several passages from the Bible. Congress eventually passed and the states ratified (in 1919) the Eighteenth Amendment outlawing the "manufacture, sale, or transportation of intoxicating liquors" throughout the United States. However, fourteen years later, in 1933, the Twenty-first Amendment reversed the earlier attempt to enshrine in our nation's laws the religious and moral objections to drinking.

What went wrong with Prohibition? On one level, we find the simple technical answer: criminalizing alcohol produces no deterrent effect on actual levels of drinking, but merely fosters greater control on the part of organized crime over this and other vices. The law also suffered from selective enforcement, as legal authorities charged with implementing the ban often looked the other way out of disinterest or because they were bribed to do so. Ultimately, what made Prohibition unworkable was its faulty underlying assumption that it is possible to legislate morality regarding behavior that much of the population considers acceptable. Most people considered drinking to excess a sin but not necessarily a crime. In the absence of a firm consensus that any drinking at all (not merely imbibing to the point of intoxication) should be criminalized, civil law turned out to be too blunt an instrument to enlist in this battle against immorality. Paradoxically, the temperance crusade was perhaps the most *intemperate* social movement in U.S. history. Its insistence that we should all be teetotalers turned out to be an unrealistic expectation when it confronted the actual realities of law enforcement and public opinion.

The lessons we should learn from the brief experiment with Prohibition are clear. Beware of the religiously inspired crusading spirit, for it tempts us to forget some important commonsense considerations. No matter how persuasive and desirable a given cause for social improvement might appear, it is still necessary to consider all the relevant political realities, including the likely consequences of making sweeping changes in public policy. Even if religious or humanitarian arguments convince us that the world would be a better place if a given vice or pattern of human behavior were eliminated, it is still wise to retain a healthy skepticism about "social engineering" of any stripe, no matter how sincerely motivated.

Religious Idealism: Its Contribution to Politics

The world of politics is an arena dominated by the necessity of compromise and mutual adjustment to opposing voices. Even when we can muster a majority, it is important to consider the opinions of the minority and consult broadly before acting through the political process. A crusading spirit often precludes the prudence necessary for wise governance. Does this leave any room at all for religious contributions to public policy debates? It certainly does. Religion offers one thing the political process requires but can find in no other place: ideals.

It is no embarrassment to say that religion offers politics the perspective of a utopia, a place that does not actually exist but nevertheless provides us with standards for judging the political order that does exist. Under the influence of theological principles and the religious imagination, people of faith have consistently supplied ordinary politics with indispensable portrayals of ideal order, virtues, and pure motivation that have served the common good in many cultures and contexts. Religions lend these ideals to the political order in various ways. Religious institutions (churches, mosques, synagogues, faith-based nonprofit organizations) witness to ideals by living out values such as love and compassion, thereby setting an example for others. Religious leaders and intellectuals share ideals by knowing and exposing sources of social wisdom contained in their traditions of reflection upon life in society. This is precisely the purpose of contemporary Catholic social teaching in all it says about peace, justice, and social cooperation for the common good.

The one thing that remains "out of bounds" for religious leaders as they aspire to share the utopian ideals of their visions of proper social ordering is any direct attempt to control the social order by actually wielding political power.

Holding political office or overseeing the actual making of laws in the name of your religion is usually understood to be overstepping the proper boundaries between faith and politics. "Jerusalem" has a legitimate role in advising "Athens" but should not rob "Athens" of its proper authority. Excessive entanglement in the political process on the part of religious leaders would be as inappropriate as a coach or team chaplain jumping off the bench and running onto the playing field, a place where such figures do not belong during the game.

There is a legitimate autonomy of the secular realm that must be respected if religious leaders are to remain true to their mission. Recognizing this truth was a significant contribution of the Second Vatican Council (or Vatican II for short) to the Catholic understanding of the role of politics in our complex, pluralistic world. Vatican II was a worldwide gathering of church leaders who met in Rome during the early 1960s. One of the final documents it approved is entitled "Pastoral Constitution on the Church in the Modern World," often known by its first three words in Latin, *Gaudium et Spes*. In paragraph 36 of this document, the Council Fathers affirm that there is a "rightful independence of earthly affairs" which the Church must respect. In recognizing the limits to direct church control of these areas, Vatican II echoes the exhortation of Jesus to render unto Caesar the things that belong to Caesar.

This insight applies to the realms of science, the arts, and all fields of secular learning, as well as politics. The proper division of labor affects the overall relationship between clergy and laity as well as between church and state. As that same Vatican II document states in paragraph 43:

> Let the lay [people] not imagine that [their] pastors are always such experts, that to every problem that arises, however complicated, they can readily give [them] a concrete solution, or even that such is their mission.

Religious values in general, and the moral teachings of the Church in particular, are to serve as important guides to the political activities of lay Christians and others, but ultimately the political world operates in ways that are independent of religious authority.

A Delicate Balance

In noting the distinctions between the world of faith and the arena of politics, the paragraphs immediately above may give the impression that we have slid into the sectarian position, the "either/or" option where faith and culture are radically at odds and the best response for people of sincere faith is to live apart from secular society. Upon closer inspection, however, that is not at all the message of Catholic social teaching, even in those moments when it acknowledges the necessity of some degree of separation between faith and secular culture. Nowhere in the Church's teaching on social issues is there any approval for a sectarian option. Neither papal encyclicals nor statements of bishops offer encouragement to those who, like the Amish, decide to insulate themselves from the modern world for the purpose of preserving their own personal purity from the threat of secular infection.

The contemporary Church has consistently called upon Catholics to practice social responsibility by involving themselves in the messy world of politics and modern culture, to engage in serious efforts to improve today's world. For the most part, in fact, the Church identifies *apathy* as the most pressing enemy of proper social engagement. This word refers to our hesitation to get sufficiently involved in worldly affairs, a temptation that leads us to set our aspirations for social improvement too low.

When the Church does, on occasion, sound warnings about inappropriate involvements in politics, it is merely attempting to navigate the tricky waters of defining its overall mission in a proper and balanced way. While the struggle for social justice will remain an indispensable part of the

Church's work for as long as we inhabit a world marked by sin, the mission of the Church can never be reduced to this one aspect. The essential task entrusted to the Church is to evangelize—to preach the Word of God and to proclaim God's kingdom to a world in need of hope. There will always be a delicate balance between the two places where this hope is found: the hope that lies in *human history,* and the hope that lies in the *Kingdom of God.*

We must never forget these two locations of hope, for there is no substitute for either one. If all our hope is found in the kingdom, then our focus becomes too *other-worldly* and we are tempted to cease caring about social issues. We are at risk of spiritualizing away the real-life issues of grinding material poverty and injustice that threaten the lives of millions in need of liberation and opportunity. But if all our hope becomes *this-worldly* and focuses on human history, we are in danger of losing our perspective on the ultimate meaning of earthly existence and forgetting the eternal life of grace that is our supernatural destiny. Remembering that we are citizens of heaven before we are citizens of any earthly society is an indispensable task of our Christian identity. This awareness has the beneficial effect of relativizing our secular loyalties and placing into perspective all our human endeavors, including our work for social improvement.

Since the very dawn of Christianity, theologians have addressed the complex relationship between human history and God's kingdom. Today we join those who have gone before us in asking questions such as: Is the kingdom already somehow present among us, as Jesus proclaimed? If so, can our efforts do anything to bring the kingdom closer, or does such talk somehow amount to blasphemy or idolatry? Does our work for social justice have any bearing on the unfolding of salvation history, the process of human redemption and ultimate reconciliation with God?

Many answers to these mysteries have been proposed, but the best responses are those in which the dual nature of the human person is always prominent. Each human person is simultaneously a body and a soul; our material and spiritual aspects are inseparable and are united in a mysterious and holy way. As humans beings, we can never be reduced merely to our bodies, nor can we be understood as disembodied souls. Any responsible theology must consider, with the utmost seriousness, both aspects of our reality. To truly respect people is to demonstrate concern for their earthly well-being as well as their heavenly destiny. We must be careful to avoid straying into either extreme: the exclusively this-worldly approach and the exclusively other-worldly approach. Responsible evangelization will always display these two faces, balancing them carefully so that neither human dimension is denigrated. Church activity must always include social action to make life on earth more humane, but it must never become so politicized that it loses sight of our transcendent purpose.

Together on Pilgrimage

The history of Christianity is full of attempts to address the proper balance between these extremes. Some of these attempts turned out to be false starts or dead ends—theologies that distorted the proper relationship between the material and the spiritual realms and often ended up being recognized as heretical once their shortcomings were exposed. Perhaps the most helpful approach to this bundle of mysteries is summarized in a simple metaphor that has at once consoled and challenged millions of Christians over the years: the metaphor of *pilgrimage*. By recognizing themselves as a "pilgrim people," members of the Christian community have developed a useful language for speaking about the significance of the present world as well as the Kingdom of God— our ultimate destination. The importance of each world is neither exaggerated nor neglected, for pilgrims are concerned about both the end point of their journey as well as the conditions along the way.

Like all travelers, pilgrims experience a dual identity. They feel deeply connected to the road they walk even as they feel in their hearts that they belong to the holy place they approach. The twin memberships may cause considerable tension but, at its best, this is a creative tension, one that continually allows pilgrims to experience a true unity of intention and purpose. The light that reaches their eyes from the heavens does not distract them from their earthly journey but, rather, illumines the path they walk toward their destination. With faith in God and goodwill in their hearts, Christian pilgrims have discovered within themselves the energy and motivation to give their full attention to the deliberate action of walking along the way of life. They nurture the hope that, by working together to improve the present age, the ultimate justice of God's kingdom will be reflected a bit more clearly through the attainment of greater social justice in the world we share.

The wonders of this simple metaphor explain why it has played so prominent a role in Christian reflection on the meaning of earthly existence in many ages. It guided St. Augustine in writing *The City of God*, his attempt to explain the significance of Christian faith in the context of the late Roman Empire; it was used by St. Thomas Aquinas and

Martin Luther in their distinctive approaches to the challenges of living an authentic Christian life in their own centuries; and it guided the Second Vatican Council as it grappled with the realities of a rapidly changing global society with an ambiguous relationship to Christian faith.

This metaphor of pilgrimage forms a helpful backdrop for serious reflection about the social mission of the Church in our new millennium as well. It allows us to view the world of politics and the secular culture around us in a new light—not as hostile territory to be conquered or shunned but, rather, as a privileged place along our way, perhaps even as a place where we may encounter the God of our longings in the multiple environments of our daily living.

Questions for Reflection

1. Have you ever felt tension between being a citizen and being a disciple? At what times and on what issues did these tensions arise?

2. Do you know anyone whose life is lived, in part or in full, according to the "sectarian option"? Have you ever had a conversation with others about the difficulty of reconciling modern secular culture with your life of faith?

3. Can you think of additional examples from history when religion played an excessive or exaggerated public role? Were the lessons available from these episodes at all different from the examples we saw (the Crusades, Manifest Destiny, Prohibition) in this chapter?

4. Do you agree that it is important to have a vision of Utopia? How does possessing a picture of an ideal order assist us in participating in the politics of everyday life?

5. Which temptation are you more apt to fall into: an excess of *this-worldly* aspirations or of *other-worldly* spirituality? Do you find the Catholic Church's statements leaning too far to either side of this spectrum for your comfort?

Chapter 3

How We Inherited the Tradition of Catholic Social Teaching

In the previous two chapters, we explored some of the pressing questions that arise when religious people reflect on the implications of their faith for the way they live in society. Left on their own to tackle these questions, individual Christians would have nearly a full-time job discerning the "signs of the times," trying to interpret contemporary events in the light of the gospel, and attempting to balance all the conflicting messages. This could lead to ceaseless worries about a number of hard questions: On which key problems of the day should I make an effort to stay informed? Am I placing too much hope in history, or perhaps not enough, in my approach to social issues? What balance should I, as a disciple and as a citizen, strike between charity and justice on any given issue? Am I guilty of an excessively crusading spirit, or am I perhaps becoming too apathetic about contributing to public dialogue and action to combat injustices? Might my habitual approach to public affairs result in "Jerusalem" saying too much or perhaps too little to "Athens"?

This chapter comes as good news for those who feel weighed down by the burden of grappling with such questions. The message of this chapter is that much of the "homework" and "legwork" have already been done on our behalf. Over the past century or so, the Church has developed a body of social teachings that contains immense wisdom. In a dozen major documents, popes, bishops, and other church leaders share valuable reflections on the intersection between faith and politics. On the national, regional, and worldwide levels, the Catholic Church is seriously committed to providing leadership and assistance to all Christians who seek to develop an authentic faith-based response to changing political, social, and economic conditions.

The Documentary Heritage

Table 1 (see page 78) contains a list of twelve documents of the universal church. Ten of these documents were published by various popes who served since the end of the nineteenth century. Most documents in this category are referred to as "encyclicals," substantial writings (often fifty pages or more) that appear in the form of letters and are intended to circulate widely among members of the Church. Recent popes have published dozens of encyclicals on many topics, but the list in Table 1 contains only the ones considered to be "social encyclicals." While almost any writing signed by a pope has some social implications, these particular encyclicals are primarily concerned with the challenges of political and economic life in the contemporary world.

For your convenience, Table 1 lists the Latin title and its usual English translation, followed by its year of publication and the name of the pope responsible for it. Encyclicals are usually divided into sections or chapters, and citations from them usually mention the standard paragraph numbers that appear in the original Latin text of each document. Table 1 attempts to situate each document in its historical context by summarizing the key social challenges facing the Church at that moment. Finally, Table 1 summarizes how each document responded to that challenge by listing the most memorable new message or idea contained in that document.

Note that Table 1 includes two social teaching documents that do not come exclusively from popes. One of them is *Gaudium et Spes*. As we noted in chapter two, this wide-ranging document of social teaching was approved in 1965 by the Second Vatican Council, a worldwide church gathering that included cardinals, bishops, and other church officials along with Pope Paul VI who presided over the final session of the council. Also appearing in Table 1 is *Justitia in Mundo*, ("Justice in the World"), a document from the worldwide Synod of Bishops held in Rome in 1971. As its title indicates, this document (by far the shortest one on this list) deals with the theme of global social justice and certainly belongs among the key social teaching documents.

When people talk about Catholic social teaching, they are usually referring to these twelve documents. Each document breaks new ground by introducing original concepts and novel ways of thinking about economic and political challenges of its day. But there is also a broader interpretation of what counts as Catholic social teaching and where it is located. A careful observer of Vatican affairs will note the huge number of other occasions when church officials speak out on public issues. For example, whenever a pope gives a speech, sermon, or interview, whether in Rome or while traveling around the globe, there is a built-in opportunity to address social, political, and economic matters.

In addition, several Vatican offices, commissions, congregations, and secretariats regularly issue statements that include at least some messages with public import. Particularly influential in this regard is the Vatican Secretariat of State, which represents the Vatican at international conferences and maintains diplomatic relations with most nations in the world. Another important player is the Papal Commission on Justice and Peace, a distinguished group of scholars, bishops, and other church officials who are charged with numerous projects, giving the commission an active presence in international circles of social concern.

An additional component of the broader heritage of church social teaching comes not from the Vatican at all but from the 108 regular local gatherings of bishops in every nation or region around the world. When bishops of a given area meet on a regular basis, they are referred to as an "episcopal conference." In most nations with a significant number of Catholics, the bishops within the nation will meet, at least annually, to coordinate church life. This task includes both internal church matters, such as initiatives on liturgical texts, religious education, and the training of clergy, and external social issues on which the Church is called to show forth its public face and speak out on important political matters, such as peace, justice, and human rights. The importance of the contributions of these national or regional meetings was reaffirmed during the 1960s, as a greater appreciation of how bishops could share their teaching mission developed. The word *collegiality* describes this growing desire for cooperation among bishops on a level above that of individual dioceses, and the necessity for collaboration among groups of bishops is mentioned often in the New Code of Canon Law published in 1983.

The bishops of the United States have been meeting in one form or another since the 1880s. The American bishops now number over two hundred and include ordinaries (the main bishop who oversees a diocese) and auxiliary bishops from all fifty states. They gather two times a year, usually in Washington, D.C., under the name "National Conference of Catholic Bishops," often shortened to the "Bishops' Conference" or simply abbreviated as the NCCB. Assisted by their professional staff in Washington, the bishops divide their work among numerous committees, several of which concentrate on social issues. Over the past few decades, the NCCB has written and approved (usually by nearly unanimous votes) many documents on public affairs. In the context of the life of the Catholic community in the United States, these bishops' statements are rightly considered to be an important part of Catholic social teaching.

Most noteworthy among the major pastoral letters of the NCCB are the 1983 letter "The Challenge of Peace: God's Promise and Our Response" and the 1986 statement "Economic Justice for All: Pastoral Letter on Catholic Social Teaching and the U.S. Economy." While the episcopal conferences of many other nations have issued their own statements on similar topics of peace and justice, these are the two most significant letters that have influenced public debate within and beyond the Catholic community in the United States.

These, then, are the sources of official Catholic social teaching: papal encyclicals, statements of Vatican offices and commissions, church councils, and episcopal conferences of bishops. Beyond these, some church observers call attention to several other sources of unofficial (but nonetheless authentic) Catholic social teaching. While only popes, bishops, and those they specifically delegate for the task of clarifying doctrine can be said to have formal teaching authority (the Latin word for this is *magisterium*) in the Church, there is a related authority that we can readily see in upstanding Catholics who interpret and put into practice the words of the magisterium. Some of these are members of the clergy and some are lay men and women. Since so few Catholics ever get around to reading lengthy and complex social teaching documents, it naturally happens that the task of spreading the Church's social message falls to people on the local level. They are practitioners—people whose activities complement the efforts of theorists of Catholic social teaching.

When a parish priest preaches an especially passionate sermon on social justice, when a lay editor of a diocesan newspaper writes an effective column about our moral obligations to the poor, when a director of religious education for a wealthy parish courageously adopts a curriculum encouraging greater sharing of resources, when a deacon commits himself to visiting prisons or city hospitals more often: these are the ways in which Catholic social teaching is spread in everyday life. Theologians, parish-based community organizers, and Catholic labor union advocates also make their own distinctive contributions, often doing things that bishops and popes would do if they had the time, expertise, and local contacts.

Of course, none of these everyday contributions takes away the need for theological reflection and publishing documents at the highest levels of our Church. Yet noting the necessity for grassroots contributions does serve as a needed reminder that there is more to doing justice than merely talking about it and writing learned encyclicals. Surely some of the most courageous advocates of peace and justice in our day have indeed been popes and bishops with formal teaching authority. It is also true, however, that among the most recognizable voices of Catholic social teaching have been several beloved figures—Mother Teresa of Calcutta, Lech Walesa, and Dorothy Day, among others—who were representatives of unofficial but truly authentic church-based reflection on social justice.

A Look Back to the Nineteenth Century

So far this chapter has focused on the *form* that official Catholic social teaching takes. We get a closer look at the actual *content* of this teaching in chapter five, which is dedicated to a thorough examination of its major themes. But to gain an initial appreciation of the change over time in the content of that teaching, let us conduct a brief "thought experiment." Note that the first modern social encyclical, the first item in Table 1, was Pope Leo XIII's encyclical letter *Rerum Novarum*, ("The Condition of Labor") published in 1891. The concepts discussed by Pope Leo had developed gradually within the consciousness of church leaders over the previous fifty years or so. Because each of the subsequent documents in Table 1 gradually brought us closer to where the Church stands today on social, political, and economic issues, let us conduct a comparison between the social message the official Catholic Church might have professed in, say, the year 1841, and what we have come to expect it to say today.

We start with the present, situated as we are in the early years of the new millennium. First consider this question: If you were told that the Pope has just released a new social encyclical and that a one-page summary of this new encyclical will appear on the third page of tomorrow morning's newspaper, what would you expect to read when you picked up that paper and turned to page three? Would you not expect several mentions of phrases such as "human rights," "equality between all peoples," "social justice," and "peace and reconciliation"? Would you not expect any new encyclical to contain words challenging us to build bridges toward those who are different from us, to advance the cause of human freedom, to make sacrifices for the less fortunate, to promote social change that would create new opportunities for people of all nations, and to denounce the injustice of extreme inequalities in wealth and income?

These themes have indeed been among the dominant messages in the last several decades of Catholic social teaching and will surely continue to play a prominent role in the Church's social documents in our new century. The Vatican

II document *Gaudium et Spes* summarizes these typical concerns of recent social teaching when it boldly declares:

> . . . with respect to the fundamental rights of the person, every type of discrimination, whether social or cultural, whether based on race, sex, color, social condition, language, or religion, is to be overcome or eradicated as contrary to God's intent (no. 29).

However, it was not always this way. Even if we went back to *Rerum Novarum* in 1891, we would find little support for the notion of equality among all people. But let us go back even further, to 1841, to those years before the Church began to wake up to the call to advance social justice (a term rarely used before 1931). In the early decades of the nineteenth century, the Catholic Church was very much a European-dominated church, one where Latin was spoken in liturgy and church affairs, and where nostalgia for premodern customs was prevalent. There was little sensitivity among Vatican officials, or even among most missionaries, to the riches of non-Western cultures or the needs and vulnerabilities of the less-developed and colonized lands of Africa, Asia, and Latin America. The concerns of church leaders were dominated by the political situation in Europe, a continent that was still recovering from the upheaval of the French Revolution and the turmoil of the Napoleonic wars.

Having been stripped of so much land and so many privileges during the French Revolution, and having lost so much prestige in its aftermath, the Catholic Church struck a reactionary posture, deeply suspicious of modernizing political and economic trends and new ways of thought. The Church in the middle of the nineteenth century saw the wealthy elites of Europe, especially the royal and aristocratic families, as its only allies in a politically dangerous world. It became an outspoken opponent of social change, including movements promising greater freedoms and benefits to workers. Many church leaders yearned for a return to the medieval order, one in which the common people of farms and villages accepted their place at the bottom of a sharply divided social ladder. In its desire for political security and a stable social order, the Church by and large opposed any secular-grounded ideas for progress and social improvement.

During those early and middle decades of the nineteenth century, church leaders took every opportunity to denounce notions such as human rights, the organization of modern labor unions, expanded freedom of speech, human equality, religious toleration, and interreligious dialogue as dangerous ideas and practices. In 1864, for example, Pope Pius IX published the famous "Syllabus of Errors," which warned Catholics against the temptations of a list of eighty errors including dozens of such modern ideas. To illustrate its

eeded an advocate, but up until that time the
been unresponsive.

efore and after his appointment as bishop in
r spearheaded a remarkable movement among
words and deeds, through direct involvement in
uggling workers as well as in sermons, speeches,
s he wrote, Ketteler inspired others to look at
new eyes. Poverty should not be viewed primar-
ament for the supposed laziness, sin, or vice of
he insisted, but rather as a result of systemic
kept wages unconscionably low and cut off the
of people from opportunities to improve their
as subsistence wages were the rule, even the
king and blameless of families would remain
cycle of desperate poverty. A large number of
cluding crime, violence, disease, and family
be remedied if the root causes of poverty were

op Ketteler was not afraid to identify the
key agent of social change. He encouraged
ganize in labor unions and other church-based
to protect their rights and promote the com-
drew inspiration from scriptural and theolog-
cluding the thirteenth-century writings of St.
as. His knowledge of the Catholic tradition

fearfulness, consider that the "Syllabus" condemns the opinion that the "Church should be separated from the state, and
the state from the Church." Instead, it insists that the
"Catholic religion should be treated as the only religion of the
state" and denies that each person "should be free to embrace
and profess the religion which he thinks to be true." Today we
not only take for granted the desirability of most of these
things once condemned by Pius IX, but the contemporary
Catholic Church is eager to support many of these very
things in its social teachings. Although we might say that the
reaction of the Church at the time may have been quite
understandable, given all that had preceded it, today we
would reach the blunt but honest conclusion that during
these decades the Church found itself squarely on the wrong
side of history.

This "thought experiment" provides two lessons. First
is the familiar insight that we should not take for granted the
state of the world as we encounter it today. Situations we consider natural and inevitable, such as the support of church
leaders for human rights, freedom, and social equality, could
well have turned out otherwise. Indeed, for most of its history, the Church frankly opposed these ideas as dangers to the
divinely ordained social order. The second lesson involves an
appreciation for what it was that changed in the course of the
nineteenth century. What social conditions or theological

principles led a pope, specifically Leo XIII, to alter the Church's stance so dramatically by the end of that century? What forces set into motion this revolutionary transformation of the Church's entire approach to social relations?

Pioneers of Social Catholicism

The answer to this last question is too complex to develop fully here, but we at least can take note of a few brave men whose efforts started movements and eventually created the momentum that led the Church to side with the underprivileged members of society rather than continuing to identify primarily with the elites of Europe.

When it began to realize the extent of daily suffering that was going on beyond the walls of the Vatican, the official Church changed its social posture. Under the guidance of a few pioneers of social concern, the Church's position on economic and political maters gradually evolved from an embattled reactionary defensiveness to a more progressive, open-minded stance that looked upon the struggles of the least advantaged workers and families with genuine concern and an eye for the structural dimensions of advancing the cause of social justice.

Who were these
influenced modern Cath
brief look at just a handf
influential person was A
Ketteler (1811–1877) o
decades of the 1800s, A
among the "Social Catho
thinkers, consisting of b
nized great potential for
industrial order. With t
mechanized production
held the promise of brir
workers. Technological
be harnessed to improv
cially the millions who
ulation into the great c

But urbanization
fiting all social classes
ordinary laborers in fa
trapped in overcrowdec
access to schooling or c
were low and labor c
workdays, backbreaki
and the ever present da
alizing the workers of

desperately
Church had
Both
1850, Kette
Catholics. I
the lives of s
and the boo
poverty with
ily as a punis
an individua
injustice that
vast majority
lives. As lon
most hardwc
trapped in a
social ills, in
breakup, coul
addressed.

Archbis
Church as a
Catholics to c
lay association
mon good. H
ical sources, i
Thomas Aqui

convinced Ketteler that it was his duty as a church leader to denounce extreme inequality, unbridled competition, and misguided notions of unlimited property rights that sacrificed the legitimate needs of the community to the interests and ever greater profits of a few elite captains of industry.

During these years, other industrializing nations witnessed similar efforts on the part of key Catholic figures who sought to awaken the Church and the wider society to the true character of poverty in the new industrial order. In France, for example, the plight of the working class was championed by diverse figures who, despite a common grounding in the same Catholic faith, occupied all wings of the political spectrum. Among the most prominent was Frédérick Ozanam (1813–1853), the founder of the St. Vincent de Paul Society, a Catholic charitable organization that is still active in some 300,000 Catholic parishes around the world. A learned and affluent layman known for his frequent visits to the squalid homes of the poor of Paris and Lyons, Ozanam was extraordinarily dedicated to performing direct works of charity, even when he found himself seriously ill or preoccupied with the numerous demands of his career. Remarkably, his commitment to acts of *charity* did not prevent Ozanam from speaking forthrightly about the need also for *justice*—the necessity for serious changes in social structures to benefit the desperately poor.

Other proponents of liberty and social reform in France during these decades included Charles de Montalembert (1810–1870) and Albert de Mun (1841–1914). Each of these laymen was a talented writer, orator, and politician who moved in the inner circles of French power. Although they both grew up in aristocratic families, they came to advocate the well-being of the poor as a crucial concern of any authentic agenda of the Catholic Church.

The best representative of nineteenth-century Social Catholicism in England was Cardinal Henry Edward Manning (1808–1892). First in his private reflections as a young man, and later in his capacity as the Catholic Archbishop of London, Manning considered it a serious and ominous omission that so few Catholics were concerned about the problems of exploited factory workers. He was worried that atheistic socialism would begin to appeal to the dockworkers and factory employees he came to know personally. This concern would become even more of a threat if the Church continued to be perceived as indifferent to their demands for better treatment.

Besides fervently speaking out about social injustices, Manning performed many symbolic and substantial deeds to demonstrate his concern for the poor and his desire to awaken rich Catholics out of their slumber of apathy. In the

1860s he canceled plans to build a new Westminster cathedral so the money could be used to open over twenty new schools for children in poor families. He consistently supported labor unions, workers' rights, and new social legislation that would benefit the working class, insisting that government agencies should shoulder some social obligation to assist the destitute.

All of these leaders of Social Catholicism in Europe played a role, directly or indirectly, in the birth of modern Catholic social teaching. They prepared the way for the definitive moment when the official Catholic Church would stand up for the rights of workers and issue a formal protest against the starvation wages that threatened the very lives of millions of workers and their families. Those of us today who are proud of the tradition of Catholic social teaching owe a great debt of gratitude to all the laity and clergy of previous centuries who, by their words and deeds, nudged the Church closer to the socially responsible stance we too often take for granted. No one deserves our praise more than Archbishop Ketteler, who planted so many of the seeds of reform, and Cardinal Manning, who was fortunate to live just long enough to witness the adoption of his proposals for worker justice by Pope Leo XIII in his issuing of the first social encyclical, *Rerum Novarum*, in 1891.

The Writing
of the Social Encyclicals

Each of the twelve major documents of Catholic social teaching deserves careful study and analysis, for each is a unique contribution with a distinctive message. In these pages we will not march through the list of all twelve documents to investigate what makes each encyclical special. Entire books have been dedicated to this task, some of which are listed in the "For Further Study" section (page 241). Rather, the remainder of this chapter explores some of the central questions regarding what the documents have in common and how we might understand the historical unfolding of the tradition of Catholic social teaching.

One question that naturally arises concerns the timing of new encyclicals. How does a pope decide that the time is ripe for writing and publishing a new document of social teaching? Part of the answer becomes obvious if we look closely at the list of dates for the documents contained in Table 1. It is no mere accident that so many of the social encyclicals were published on major anniversaries of *Rerum Novarum*, which appeared in 1891. The fortieth, seventieth, eightieth, ninetieth, and one hundredth anniversaries of Pope

Leo XIII's first social encyclical were marked by subsequent popes publishing new documents of social teaching. Indeed, some of the Latin titles of these documents make explicit reference to the anniversary dates. Every time we enter a year that ends in a "1," it is reasonable to expect a new social encyclical to be released, for this pattern held true in 1931, 1961, 1971, 1981, and 1991. Most of these anniversary documents spend several paragraphs in tribute to their predecessors, often explaining at length how the new teaching follows from the basic principles contained in *Rerum Novarum*.

But there is more to the timing of social encyclicals than the sheer momentum of the calendar or force of habit. Each encyclical has represented the Church's response to a specific set of events or social concerns that demanded the attention of political and religious leaders at that specific moment of history. For example, the writing of *Quadragesimo Anno* ("After Forty Years" or "The Reconstruction of the Social Order") in 1931 was prompted by a worldwide economic crisis that crushed the confidence of millions. The sudden stock market crash of 1929 and the shock of startling levels of unemployment in the early years of the Great Depression demanded a substantial response from Pope Pius XI as he agonized over the financial chaos, ruined dreams, and destitution of millions of families in Europe, America, and most other regions of the world.

Another dramatic example is Pope John XXIII's 1963 encyclical *Pacem in Terris*, ("Peace on Earth"), which included a plea for peace and disarmament just months after the Cuban Missile Crisis of 1962 threatened the world with the specter of nuclear annihilation. Further, even if 1991 had not been the one-hundredth anniversary of *Rerum Novarum*, Pope John Paul II might well have taken the opportunity to comment on the events of 1989–1990 (including the fall of the Berlin Wall, the demise of Soviet Communism, and the breakup of the USSR), as he did in *Centesimus Annus* ("On the Hundredth Anniversary of *Rerum Novarum*").

In a sense, then, each new social encyclical can be interpreted as an occasion for the Church to address the challenges of new events on the world stage. Sometimes these events are dramatic; at other times, however, they are gradual developments. Such was the case with the phasing out of colonialism, which is a major concern of *Popolorum Progressio* ("The Development of People") in 1967, or the growth of international trade, treated in *Sollicitudo rei Socialis* ("On Social Concern") in 1987. Whenever we look at a document such as the encyclicals of Catholic social teaching, it is wise to ask the revealing question: To what conditions or events is this author responding? Situating the encyclicals in their historical context is an important first step to understanding their message and significance.

While it is true that each encyclical is a response to the special political and economic challenges of its era, we must not lose track of one of the marvelous features of Catholic social teaching: the way each successive encyclical builds upon the insights of its predecessors. The documents have a wonderful way of combining the new with the old, of building novel structures upon existing foundations. The tradition renews itself by constantly considering the state of secular affairs and holding up this picture of the world to the continuous light of the gospel and Christian theology. While new times call for creative solutions that adjust to changing realities, there is also a set of core principles regarding social justice and moral obligations that should shape our actions in every age.

Scholars who trace the development of Catholic social teaching have studied this dynamic of continuity and change in the social encyclicals and have staked out various positions along a spectrum of opinions about the nature of the encyclicals. At one extreme is the idea that social and theological principles pass in an uninterrupted line from papal mind to papal mind, with a tight, organic connection between everything successive popes might say about political and economic affairs. At the other extreme is the idea that each encyclical captures only the idiosyncratic views of its author and is essentially unrelated to what came before it or will come after it.

Obviously, the truth lies somewhere between these extremes. There is substantial continuity between the messages of the popes, even when their encyclicals appear decades apart from one another. But the march of time and social progress give each successive encyclical a broader and, I would argue, a more constructive approach. The most recent documents grapple seriously with certain realities—such as the aspirations of women for social equality, the urgency of nuclear disarmament, and the need to address the painful legacies of colonialism—that the earliest documents could scarcely acknowledge. The progress of Catholic social teaching may be summarized as growth toward ever wider circles of social concern, reflecting the increase of awareness within the Church of numerous injustices that demand our attention, commitment, and action.

Questions for Reflection

1. How familiar are you with the work of the National Conference of Catholic Bishops and other national episcopal conferences? Can you list some of their functions and contributions?

2. If you had lived in the years before *Rerum Novarum* was published in 1891, would you likely have joined the effort of the early pioneers of "Social Catholicism"? Why or why not?

3. Do you see any similarities between the crisis of industrialization that the world experienced in the 1890s and the economic situations facing workers today? If so, can you recommend any messages that might be contained in a new encyclical written today that would courageously address this new phase of industrial woes, as did *Rerum Novarum* in 1891?

Table I
Major Documents of Modern Catholic Social Teaching

Latin title	English translation	Year of publication	Source
Rerum Novarum	The Condition of Labor	1891	Pope Leo XIII
Quadragesimo Anno	After Forty Years, or The Reconstruction of the Social Order	1931	Pope Pius XI
Mater et Magistra	Christianity and Social Progress	1961	Pope John XXIII
Pacem in Terris	Peace on Earth	1963	Pope John XXIII
Gaudium et Spes	Pastoral Constitution on the Church in the Modern World	1965	Second Vatican Council
Popolorum Progressio	The Development of Peoples	1967	Pope Paul VI
Octogesima Adveniens	A Call to Action on the 80th Anniversary of *Rerum Novarum*	1971	Pope Paul VI
Justitia in Mundo	Justice in the World	1971	Synod of Bishops
Evangelii Nuntiandi	Evangelization in the Modern World	1975	Pope Paul VI
Laborem Exercens	On Human Work	1981	Pope John Paul II
Sollicitudo rei Socialis	On Social Concern	1987	Pope John Paul II
Centesimus Annus	On the Hundredth Anniversary of *Rerum Novarum*	1991	Pope John Paul II

Major challenge it addressed	Major new message or idea
Industrialization, urbanization, poverty	"Family Wage," workers' rights
Great Depression, Communism, and fascist dictatorships	Subsidiarity as a guide to government interventions
Technological advances	Global justice between rich and poor nations
Arms race, the threat of nuclear war	A philosophy of human rights and social responsibilities
Younger generations questioning traditional values	Church must scrutinize external "signs of the times"
Widening gap between rich and poor nations	"Development is a new word for peace"
Urbanization marginalizes vast multitudes	Lay Catholics must focus on political action to combat injustices
Structural injustices and oppression inspire liberation movements	"Justice . . . is a constitutive dimension of the preaching of the gospel"
Cultural problems of atheism, secularism, consumerism	The salvation promised by Jesus offers liberation from all oppression
Capitalism and Communism treat workers as mere instruments of production	Work is the key to the "social question" and to human dignity
Persistent underdevelopment, division of world into blocs	"Structures of sin" are responsible for global injustices
Collapse of Communism in Eastern Europe	Combat consumeristic greed in new "knowledge economy"

Chapter 4

The Sources and Methods of Catholic Social Teaching

Catholic social teaching is just one example of a tradition of ethics. Throughout human history people all over the world have shared numerous ethical traditions that have shed light on how best to plan their lives and use limited resources in cooperation with their neighbors. They inherit this wisdom from previous generations as well as finding it in their own new experiences. Ethics almost always involves making generalizations, including laws, moral principles, and other behavioral guidelines. No matter what system of thought they espouse, people tend to look for new sources of wisdom that might help shape their actions. If a group discovers a beneficial pattern of behavior or a set of useful reflection about appropriate human activity, members of the group may write it down or find some other way of sharing it with contemporaries and future generations. This is how ethical traditions take root and grow over time.

The Four Sources of Christian Ethics

As one particular tradition of moral reflection, Christian ethics has undergone this pattern of growth over the past two thousand years. When members of the Christian community turn their energies toward the task of "doing ethics," they seek to discover the behavioral implications of their faith in God. They fervently desire to cultivate a healthy relationship with their Lord and Creator, acknowledging certain obligations toward God. Some of these are summarized in the First, Second, and Third Commandments: the call to worship and praise God, to observe the Sabbath in appropriate ways, to respect the name of the Lord, and to be mindful of all that is holy.

Simultaneously, Christians recognize certain moral duties to other creatures, for loving our neighbors follows closely from loving the God who created all that exists. We consequently desire to respect life in all its forms, to preserve the beauty of the natural environment, and to avoid all actions (such as stealing, lying, adultery, and murder) that harm other people. Many of these obligations are contained in the Fourth through Tenth Commandments. The dual obligations toward God and toward others are really part of a unified call to be loving people filled with all the virtues of generous and faithful disciples of Jesus. However convenient it may be to draw a distinction between *duties to God* and *duties toward others*, the devout Christian recognizes these obligations as cut from the same cloth, as part of a seamless response to a God whose boundless love is reflected in the goodness of all created things. There is an indivisible unity in our web of relationships that leads us to pursue love and justice toward all.

The Ten Commandments have served for thousands of years as a good summary of collective moral wisdom for communities of faith around the world, first for the Jewish people and then for Christians as well; their usefulness has never diminished. In a complex and rapidly changing world, however, it has become desirable to supplement them with other types of moral wisdom, particularly with guidelines concerning our large-scale social relations. Catholic social teaching is one such attempt to provide ethical counsel regarding just relationships in political and economic life—levels of our everyday activity that are barely mentioned in the Ten Commandments. As new documents are written and as local faith communities attempt to apply the insights of Catholic social teaching to their particular situations, the tradition of Christian ethics continues to grow and mature. We seek to improve our understanding of what actions and attitudes are required by our call to be loving and faithful disciples.

The development of Catholic social teaching is a creative process, but it is governed by certain standard approaches and development patterns. This chapter describes the pattern of how certain sources, or fonts, contribute to Catholic social teaching. As is the case in all of Christian ethics, whether Catholic or Protestant, we easily observe that the social teachings of the Church draw upon four major sources of insight that contribute to their authority and shape their conclusions: 1) revelation; 2) reason; 3) tradition; and 4) experience. Let us explore how each of these sources serves as a resource for the development of Catholic social teaching.

1. Revelation: The Role of Scripture

The word *revelation* refers to the ways God shows God's self to people. The Judeo-Christian tradition has never turned its back on the possibility that individuals might experience profound revelations from the Almighty and even receive specific messages from God in the form of mystical visions. But the standard way of speaking about revelation as a source of theology is to emphasize the guidance offered to all of us in the more public and accessible form of the Scriptures. The Bible has always been the starting point for Christian ethics. Even while they understand the significance of Scripture in slightly different ways, Christian thinkers agree that the biblical record of God's revelation must play an important role in what we as Christians say about the morality of human behavior.

There have always been differences of opinion about the precise nature of the Bible. Those who lean toward biblical fundamentalism view Scripture as an inerrant record of events and commands that come directly from God. Others emphasize the human and historical dimensions of Scripture, reminding us that both the Hebrew Scriptures and the New Testament are products of human communities, however true it is that God may be called the ultimate author. In fact, it is misleading to refer to the Bible as a single book, for it is really a collection of dozens of writings assembled over hundreds of years and only gradually winning recognition as an authoritative source of religious wisdom.

For our purposes, it suffices merely to note that morality in general, and social ethics in particular, is only a small part of the overall concerns of Scripture. It would be misleading to think of the Bible as a book of detailed rules to regulate our behavior. Even in those few passages where Scripture does offer firm moral laws, significant amounts of interpretation are required before we apply their precise prescriptions to contemporary moral life. For the most part, Scripture is a record of God's gracious ways of dealing with fallen humanity, offering successive covenants that contain the promise of redemption and salvation. When various books of the Bible address the morality of human behavior, it is in the context of an overriding concern to build a faithful relationship with God and others.

One of the key terms that applies to this picture of the universe is the notion of *justice*, the controlling concept in all our reflections on social ethics. Justice is a virtue of people who are committed to fidelity to the demands of a relationship, whether with God, other individuals, or even large groups and categories of other people. It becomes a complex task to trace notions of justice through the Bible, since the various original Hebrew and Greek words for justice have associated meanings that are broader than what we today might mean by "legal justice" or "social justice." Sometimes the original biblical terms for justice (the Hebrew *mišpāt* and *sĕdāqāh*, the Greek *dikaiosynē*) are rightly translated into English terms such as "loving-kindness," "mercy," "steadfast love," "fidelity," and "righteousness"—words that indicate multiple nuances in texts that we might have hoped would give us specific guidance on contemporary economic and political matters. Those seeking to walk the path of biblical justice soon find it converging with other paths in the faith life of Israel and the early Christian communities. Our efforts to derive practical social principles for the modern world directly from the brief mentions of justice in scriptural sources usually meet with frustration.

There are several places in Scripture, however, where our search for guidance on the topic of social justice is most likely to be fruitful. One is in the books of the Hebrew prophets. Figures such as Isaiah, Jeremiah, Amos, Hosea, and Ezekiel denounce violent and fraudulent practices that, in their lifetimes, were harming the weakest members of Israelite society—widows, orphans, the poor, the outcast. Several prophets uttered stirring words that urged the establishment of a new order of social concern and harmony. Of course, these prophets often met stiff resistance to their stern reminders that all Israelites should heed God's call to practice social justice and respect the delicate web of communal relations. The Psalms and the Book of Proverbs also portray frequent pictures of the two sides of justice: the harmony that accompanies the fulfillment of justice and the turmoil associated with its violation.

The New Testament contains the Christian Scriptures that witness to the revelation of God in the person of Jesus Christ. Many of the stories about Jesus in the four Gospels offer us glimpses of a vision of justice that is bound up with the Kingdom of God. One of the mysterious things about the kingdom as Jesus describes it is that its establishment is not portrayed as merely a future event but is also somehow already present among us. The kingdom is the power of God active in the present world, and the mercy and miraculous deeds of Jesus reveal God's love and justice.

Justice is also an important concept in the letters of St. Paul. Among Paul's central concerns is the formation of communities of covenant people, and proper relations within Christian communities are governed by justice. Although some of Paul's practical advice seems dated and less than helpful today (he accepted the institution of slavery and sharply subordinated women to men in the life of the church), his treatment of justice and related themes such as freedom and reconciliation are immensely insightful.

How do the documents of Catholic social teaching make use of Scripture? On many occasions, passages of Scripture are cited directly in the texts of encyclicals, to borrow an insight or to justify a judgment. For example, in paragraph 137 of *Quadragesimo Anno*, Pope Pius XI quotes a verse from Paul's First Letter to the Corinthians to urge us to develop bonds of solidarity, since, as Paul writes, "if [one] part suffers, all the parts suffer with it" (12:26). In other instances, biblical materials are used more indirectly to evoke a sense of urgency or obligation. For example, when Pope John Paul II (in paragraph 33 of *Sollicitudo rei Socialis*) wishes to inspire greater sharing of resources between rich and poor nations, he alludes to the familiar parable of the beggar Lazarus and the rich man who excluded him from his banquet table (see Luke 16). Although, on the surface at least, the original words of Jesus were about individual acts of charity and hospitality, this encyclical extends their significance to apply the principle of mercy to the complex world of global politics. Behind such applications of Scripture lies a confident assumption within Catholic social teaching that the word of God revealed many centuries ago still finds relevance today, even in new situations that open up entire worlds far beyond the original context of divine revelation.

2. Reason: The Natural Law

We have already noted that the Catholic tradition tends to favor a "both/and" position on many issues. Catholic theology seeks to combine concerns for both body and spirit, both heaven and earth, both natural and supernatural life, both grace and nature. Another pair of terms we seek to synthesize is reason and revelation. We acknowledge that the revealed Word of God in Scripture is a special and privileged place to encounter God and to learn God's intentions for the world. But Catholic theologians are eager to combine what they learn in the Bible with insights gained by other means of human knowledge, specifically through *human reason.*

This optimism about the operations of the human mind stands in contrast to fundamentalist Christians, whose stated policy is to follow the Bible alone. It even sets Catholics apart from many mainstream Protestants whose roots in the theology of the Reformation (primarily from Martin Luther and John Calvin) lead them to be more distrustful of the operations of the human mind, corrupted as it is likely to be by the sinful tendencies caused by the fall of Adam which, they often remind us, "darkened the mind and weakened the will."

What effect does this typical Catholic confidence in reason have on Catholic social teaching? In general, modern social encyclicals exhibit a tendency to trust solutions and strategies that we derive by applying careful rational analysis to complex problems. While it is never excluded from these Catholic texts, Scripture plays far less central a role here than it does in documents from parallel Protestant sources, such as the social teachings of the World Council of Churches or individual Protestant denominations.

One specific way of using reason in theological writings is to employ a form of argumentation called natural law reasoning. Although its influence on the documents of Catholic social teaching has been diminishing over time, natural law is still important for students of Catholic ethics to understand. Explanations of natural law have a tendency to become very technical, but the basic pattern of thought behind natural law is not at all complicated. The fundamental belief of a natural law approach to ethics is that God created the universe with certain purposes in mind. God also created humans with enough intelligence that they can use their reason to observe the natural world and make reliable judgments about God's purposes and how our behavior may cooperate with God's plans. Indeed, we have a moral obligation to make good use of our minds to figure out God's intentions and to muster the courage to act on these convictions in daily life. To ignore the law of nature, which is mysteriously inscribed in our hearts and minds, is to sin by disobeying God's will.

Normally, Christians think of God's will as coming to us through Scripture, such as the contents of the Ten Commandments. A key claim of natural law theory is that nature is another path by which we learn God's will in a less direct way than through revelation. By closely observing the structures of nature, including our own bodies and the healthy instincts and inclinations built into our minds, we gain knowledge of the natural order God intends. For example, our innate desire to preserve our lives suggests the divine prohibition against suicide and, by extension, murder and wanton destruction of wildlife. Our natural desire to live peacefully in society is cited as evidence to support all the rules of social order (to avoid stealing, lying, adultery, etc.) that contribute to social stability. Indeed, it might be argued that most of the Ten Commandments could be derived this way on the basis of natural law reasoning. This observation does not displace the need for scriptural revelation but does suggest a happy overlap between the contents of revelation and reason.

It is hard to make an airtight case for any specific activity using natural law reasoning alone. An extremist might use natural law to argue, in effect, that biology is destiny and that we may never interfere with any bodily process (including perhaps even the spread of diseases) without frustrating God's purposes. Such misinterpretations overlook an additional gift of God to every person: our endowment with intelligence that we should use to improve our lives and achieve our full potential, always within the limits of the moral law. At best, natural law assists our moral reflections by limiting the field of allowable activities and reminding us not to frustrate the intentions God encoded in nature. Natural law helps to direct our freedom in moral matters, but it does not completely determine the course of action we will choose. From natural law we might learn some reliable principles (such as "preserve life whenever possible" or "spread knowledge to the next generation"), but the hard work of sorting out the relationship between means and ends still remains to be done.

This is why natural law has sometimes been called a "skeleton law." In order to make good moral decisions about practical matters, we need to know far more than the few hints that natural law reasoning can offer us about divine purposes for the universe. In fact, one of the major objections to the use of natural law is that theologians too often attempt to use this pattern of thought to make overly specific judgments concerning worldly matters about which they know little. This serious error treats ethics as if it is more a science than an art, as if moral truths can be deduced in the same way that mathematical formulas are derived from timeless principles of logic. It also treats natural law in the wrong way, as if it were "law" in the sense of a codified body of precepts rather than what it really is—a more modest achievement of reason that discloses a limited set of standards for moral behavior.

We must not allow the potential for these misuses of natural law ethics to prevent us from employing natural law in appropriate and constructive ways. At its best, natural law is a tradition of reason that sheds much light on how we may use our divinely given gift of intelligence to discern proper courses of action. It is a wonderful resource in the fight against ethical relativism, a school of thought that disputes all claims that there is objective right and wrong in the universe. It is one thing, of course, to agree that there are some absolute truths, and quite another thing to reach agreement on precisely what those truths are. Because natural law is merely a tool for interpreting the universe, people will continue to use natural law in their own preferred ways—and will continue to reach conflicting conclusions. The final interpretation that emerges, of course, will depend on who is using that tool.

How has natural law been used in Catholic social teaching? In the earliest social encyclicals in particular, popes used natural law reasoning as the basis for criticizing unjust arrangements of property and wages. Leo XIII and Pius XI both noticed a huge gap between God's intentions for the world (that we should all share resources so that God's gifts support human flourishing) and the actual state of affairs in the modern industrial world (millions starving while only a few enjoyed luxuries). Both reached the conclusion that this violation of human dignity runs contrary to natural law.

Although both were basically conservative in temperament, their employment of natural law compelled them to call for sweeping changes in the capitalist order. They called upon governments to implement legal protections for workers, and they called upon employers to change the way wages were determined, thus giving families a chance to climb out of conditions of near starvation. Although the actual civil laws of most countries at that time did not require better treatment of workers, the natural law, as these popes interpreted it, mandated reforms. Change was necessary because God's "higher law," which stands above humanly created civil laws, demanded the preservation of life and greater respect for the aspirations of working families to live in dignity.

3. Tradition: Theological Reflection in Church Life

The third of our four sources of Christian ethics is a bit harder to pin down, but its contribution to Catholic social teaching is still important. The word *tradition* as it is used here refers to all the previous reflection on social issues that has gone on within Christian theology. This serves as a reminder that what we call "modern Catholic social teaching" is only the latest in a long line of thinking within the Church about the meaning of peace and justice. Although no social encyclicals were written or published before 1891, voices within the Church have always been active in commenting on issues of life in society, including its political and economic dimensions.

Unfortunately, many valuable contributions of priests, bishops, and active laity over the ages have been lost because they were not written down and preserved. How interesting it would be if we had a complete record of the many occasions when sermons on responsible social living were preached by clergy and when lay advisors to kings cited faith-based reasons to recommend one policy or another. When we wish to consult the Christian tradition, we are more or less limited to those few sources that happen to have been written down at the time, items such as published sermons, political treatises, and letters arguing for Christian responses to particular social challenges.

One easy way to trace the source of previous reflections on social issues is simply to check the footnotes of the twelve major social teaching documents listed in Table 1. Most of the encyclicals contain numerous references to earlier theologians and other church figures who wrote and preached about justice and related social issues. Several of the most influential figures in this regard lived during the earliest centuries of the Church. Collectively, they are referred to as the "Fathers of the Church." From the Latin root word for "father" we derive the name "Patristic," which describes the era in which they lived. Among the major Patristic figures are Clement of Alexandria, Tertullian, Basil the Great, John Chrysostom, Ambrose of Milan, Augustine of Hippo and Jerome.

Most of these men have been recognized as saints and/or doctors ("great teachers") of the Church. Writing and preaching between the second and fifth centuries of the Christian era, these theologians addressed numerous matters of church doctrine and contributed greatly to our understanding of the Holy Trinity, the identity of Jesus Christ, the sacraments, Scripture, and the mission of the Church. Part of this mission is for people of faith to play an active role in the life of the wider society. If we read the many writings left behind by the Church Fathers, we encounter much insightful advice for Christians trying to live a life of faith amidst the challenges of a politically and economically divided world.

When we read Patristic literature, we might be dissatisfied with some of its positions on social issues. They may seem at first blush to be overly simplified and, therefore, largely irrelevant to the complexities of our modern era. For example, on the issue of private property, several of the Church Fathers wrote angry denunciations of greed and selfishness but did not pay sufficient attention to the detailed arguments supporting the continued recognition of private ownership of property. Basil the Great, for example, preached a famous sermon in which he boldly stated that all our surplus wealth belongs to the needy and should be distributed to the poor immediately. John Chrysostom went so far as to advocate a form of communism when he wrote: "For 'mine' and 'thine'—those chilly words which introduce innumerable wars into the world—should be eliminated . . . The poor would not envy the rich, because there would be no rich. Neither would the poor be despised by the rich, for there would be no poor. All things would be in common."

Here as elsewhere, the Fathers brilliantly advance our understanding of the social implications of the faith that come to us from Scripture, but do not succeed as well in offering us practical steps to improve society. That is why their social messages are cited by popes in recent social encyclicals primarily as reminders of basic religious virtues such as generosity and selflessness, but not as offering complete and sufficient blueprints for life in society.

The task of better bringing together the ideals of our faith with the practical demands of the everyday world fell to a later group of Christian theologians who wrote extensively on social issues—the Scholastics ("school men") of medieval Europe. The towering figure among all the Scholastics was St. Thomas Aquinas, a thirteenth-century Dominican priest and scholar who is quoted frequently in the modern social encyclicals. Aquinas had an extraordinary eye for finding ways to merge and reconcile many traditions of thought into a unified whole, or synthesis. His works, such as the masterful *Summa Theologica*, build upon the traditions of ancient Greek and Roman scholars as well as Scripture and the writings of the Patristic era and the intervening centuries. Aquinas had quite a knack for summarizing the major arguments on controversial issues and applying carefully drawn principles to reach clear and moderate conclusions grounded in reason.

For example, on the issue of private ownership of property, Aquinas affirms the wisdom of the very insights we saw above from Basil and Chrysostom, but he uses a natural law argument to moderate the force of these Patristic insights. He first recognizes that God does intend humans to share equitably in the common gifts of creation; concern for the common good, therefore, demands a broad distribution of resources so that no one is cut off from access to social participation and the means to a good livelihood. But Aquinas also recognizes the fallen nature of humanity, which makes *total* sharing of resources unlikely to work out for practical reasons. As a keen observer of human nature (and as a member of a religious order in which he had to share small rooms, scarce books, and tools), Aquinas knew that problems such as laziness, the human tendency to shirk unpleasant work, and the likelihood of disputes over shared property justify some division of goods.

While common use of all things is a laudable goal and perhaps indeed the original intention of the Creator, for Aquinas the institution of private ownership of goods is a necessary social principle in a fallen world. As a great forger of compromises, Aquinas does not really refute the Patristic sources he cites but, rather, concedes that their insights about sharing apply to the *use* of goods we all need, not to their actual *ownership*. This distinction (Scholastics loved to make distinctions) between the *use* and the *ownership* of material goods has found its way into several of the documents of modern Catholic social teaching.

Besides property, another fine case study in the growth of traditions of Christian social thought concerns the use of deadly force. Most New Testament references to violence contain blanket prohibitions against harming others for any reason whatsoever. In fact, it was common practice for the earliest Christian communities to be strictly pacifist, avoiding military service as a matter of principle and even refusing to defend themselves when captured or attacked during the Roman persecutions. By the fifth century, a few Patristic voices distanced themselves from this uncompromising position on nonresistance to evil. Most notable was St. Augustine of Hippo, a great scholar who supported a policy of using military force when absolutely necessary to preserve order. On a number of occasions, Augustine cited arguments to justify armed interventions for good causes, including the suppression of several dangerous heresies that threatened the local Church in North Africa where he served as bishop.

By making carefully reasoned arguments for the limited use of force, Augustine became a founder of the tradition of just-war theory. Later Christian authors such as Aquinas and Francisco Suarez (a seventeenth-century Jesuit theologian) expanded the reflections of Augustine and derived a list of several strict conditions under which defensive wars might be justified. This list of appropriate criteria, despite having no clear basis in Scripture, has become an accepted part of modern Catholic social teaching. Just-war theory is mentioned in several of the papal social encyclicals and is treated at length in the U.S. bishops' pastoral letter "The Challenge of Peace."

Because Scripture has always served as the starting point for Christian theological reflection, there is an especially intimate connection between Scripture and tradition, our first and third sources of Christian ethics. The Vatican II document *Dei Verbum* ("Dogmatic Constitution on Divine Revelation") speaks movingly of the close relationship between these two fonts of Catholic theology. This document points out that:

> . . . both of them (Scripture and tradition), flowing
> from the same divine wellspring, in a certain way
> merge into a unity and toward the same end (no. 9).

Our respect for Scripture and tradition cannot be separated. As key sources of Christian ethics, they work together to help believers know and interpret the word of God as it addresses our world today.

4. Experience: Engaging in Social Analysis

The last of our four sources is in a sense already contained in each of the first three. It would be impossible to talk about revelation, reason, or tradition without presuming an important role for human *experience*. Every idea a human talks about, writes down, and hands on to the next generation first passes through his or her five senses and should be considered part of human experience. In the world of social ethics, however, the word *experience* has come to mean something quite specific. In the brief section below, we describe the process of social analysis as it contributes the "experience" dimension to Catholic social teaching.

Part of the task of Catholic social teaching is to help people of faith read and interpret "the signs of the times."

This is a phrase that appears in the Gospel of Matthew (see 16:3) as well as in paragraph 4 of the Vatican II document *Gaudium et Spes*. But just how does this "reading" take place? The shortest answer to this question is to observe a common pattern that effective people follow when they meet a new situation. First they take a careful look at the situation; next they make an accurate judgment about what is going on and how best to respond to it; and finally they act vigorously upon what they have learned. This three-step process, abbreviated as "see–judge–act," has long been useful in church circles, not only in large-scale social matters but also in the spiritual discernment of individuals and small groups, as people seek to harvest the fruits of both contemplation and action in their lives. The three steps are described in some detail in paragraphs 236–241 of *Mater et Magistra* ("Christianity and Social Progress"), Pope John XXIII's 1961 encyclical.

A slightly more elaborate version of this process is outlined in a four-step schema that is usually called the "pastoral circle." Because theologians have a fondness for fancy labels, the terms "circle of praxis" and the "hermeneutical circle" have also been used to describe this method of understanding and acting on worldly realities. Whatever name we use, this process emphasizes the relationship between action and reflection and includes these four steps: 1) experience;

2) social analysis; 3) theological reflection; and 4) pastoral planning. Although the phrase "social analysis" often gets the most attention, each of these steps is a necessary part of engaging in church-based efforts for social justice. Let us look at each stage or "moment" of the circle.

1. Experience: The first step involves the initial gaining of experience itself. This requires insertion into a local situation and gathering data about social problems and their effects. It goes without saying that a certain amount of courage is necessary to get involved in controversial issues and perhaps even to find ourselves in dangerous places. But there is no substitute for leaving our armchairs and "getting our hands dirty" in real situations that affect the lives of many. If we never leave our comfortable cocoons, we deprive ourselves of the very experience upon which the pastoral circle is based.

2. Social analysis: The second step is the least obvious but perhaps the most crucial part of the circle, for only when we engage in serious social analysis can we understand all the factors behind a given social situation. Social analysis means asking hard questions about the causes of injustices and the connections between issues, as we seek to discover who is really responsible "behind the scenes" for social problems and what systems or patterns of activity perpetuate them. This second step may require the assistance of outside experts who can apply their specialized knowledge in fields such as sociology, anthropology, economics, political science, and even psychology. A good piece of advice at this stage is to retain a healthy sense of skepticism about much of what we are told, since preferred ways of seeing the world often greatly vary. The wisest course of action is to insist on hearing all sides of the story before drawing any firm conclusions. It is extremely important to make our own independent and critical judgments, because the whole process could be defeated by giving in to a misleading interpretation at this stage.

3. Theological reflection: This step accompanies social analysis and, along with it, gives us the tools to make proper judgments about social realities. Acknowledging this third stage serves as a reminder that the experiences we gain and the data we collect must also be viewed in the light of the living faith, as the Word of God and the theological tradition is brought to bear on contemporary situations. It is here that the documents of Catholic social teaching may be most useful, as they open up new insights and raise new questions we may otherwise overlook. While the other three stages of the circle emphasize our own initiatives as active participants, this stage invites us to combine our own creative thinking with a solid commitment to consult established sources of Christian social wisdom, such as the riches of Scripture, reason, and tradition we encountered above.

4. Pastoral planning: This step asks us to respond to our new knowledge by charting a course of action to guide us in preparing for the future. This is where the hard work of the earlier three stages pays off, for it allows us to reach informed decisions and choose effective strategies. The goal is to design programs of action that, by taking advantage of previous experience and reflection upon the lessons of the past, will be more helpful in meeting upcoming challenges. The pastoral circle is completed when we are able to return to the experience or insertion phase equipped with what we have learned from the journey so far.

This "experience" dimension of social ethics makes an even greater contribution when we envision this process not merely as a one-time episode but as an ongoing process of learning more and more about our world and seeking to act ever more effectively based on our increasing knowledge. Ideally, the fruitfulness of all our future efforts will benefit from past and present learnings. If we emphasize the increasing possibilities of this process, we will recognize that, when it succeeds, the pastoral circle is not a circle at all but a spiral ascending upward. At the end of each project we do not really return to where we started but, rather, find ourselves in a higher location, better informed about our social context and better prepared to take effective action in the next round of involvement.

Universal Principles and Local Applications

In the 1971 Catholic social teaching document *Octogesima Adveniens* ("A Call to Action on the 80th Anniversary of *Rerum Novarum*"), Pope Paul VI offers important advice about how we might make use of the Church's reflections on justice, peace, and life in society:

> In the face of such widely varying situations, it is difficult for us to utter a unified message and to put forward a solution which has universal validity. Such is not our ambition, nor is it our mission. It is up to the Christian communities to analyze with objectivity the situation which is proper to their own country, to shed on it the light of the Gospel's unalterable words and to draw principles of reflection, norms of judgment and directives for action from the social teaching of the church (no. 4).

Those three sentences contain much wisdom, and the message of this chapter places us in a position to understand and benefit from the words of Pope Paul VI. This chapter introduces us to the major sources and methods which contribute to the documents of Catholic social teaching. The remaining questions to consider here are: 1) How are we to combine the four sources of Christian ethics in responding to the social issues of our day? and 2) How are we to apply the rich insights of Catholic social teaching that come to us from Vatican documents to local circumstances?

When he upholds the role of local Christian communities in social action, Pope Paul VI demonstrates, in the above quotation, a solid appreciation for the "division of labor" portrayed in the pastoral circle. After all, three of the four "moments" of the circle describe activities that unfold almost exclusively on the local level. When a parish, diocese, or other religious organization undertakes a new community involvement, reflects on its effectiveness, and updates its program planning, very little conscious attention to the documents of Catholic social teaching is likely. No pope or Vatican commission has time to serve as a consultant to a local Catholic school, soup kitchen, or counseling center, even if given the opportunity to contribute through active participation. The bulk of the work, in both the reflection and the action phases, must be done on the grassroots level.

This is the very same insight contained in Pope Paul VI's words. The center of gravity in social ministries must lie with the local communities of Christians who find themselves facing a great variety of challenging social conditions. They are the ones who most often engage in the three-fold task of seeing, judging, and acting. The "seeing" and "acting" will never be able to move forward on a worldwide level. As the Pope affirms, it is difficult for any Vatican voice to address the diverse social problems of all corners of the world simultaneously by proposing detailed solutions that pretend to have universal validity. However, it is in that middle stage of "judging" where Catholic social teaching makes its great contribution.

How is this so? Recall that the four-part pastoral circle suggests that "judging" includes two components: 1) social analysis, which relies on secular fields of study such as sociology and economics; and 2) theological reflection, which relies on tools provided by the Christian tradition, such as Catholic social teaching. There are, of course, some things church documents can never do. For example, they cannot substitute for the wisdom of many years of "life experience," nor replace our vigorous efforts to forge the best possible analysis of a local social situation. This is why Pope Paul VI reminds us that universal messages from Rome cannot supply all the wisdom a Christian community might need to meet its local challenges.

But the teachings of the universal church do have an indispensable role to play in offering us general principles regarding the attainment of justice and peace. Vatican social encyclicals do much of the necessary "homework" for us in advance. Their descriptions of the meaning of common good, solidarity, freedom, and other social virtues inspire us to strive for improvement in the life of our own local communities. Reading these documents connects us to Scripture and church tradition, giving us many important tools to guide our own judgments and to apply God's summons to live justly in our daily lives. In the next chapter, we examine nine of the major themes treated in the Church's social encyclicals.

Questions for Reflection

1. Of the four sources of Christian ethics, is there one you particularly favor or disfavor? What are the reasons for your enthusiasm or reservations?

2. In describing how the four sources are sometimes combined, this chapter examines two examples of social teaching topics: ownership of private property and the just-war theory. List some other social issues on which the Church has spoken, and discuss the relative weight

given to each of the four sources in developing this teaching?

3. Have you ever engaged in a project which, knowingly or not, followed the pastoral circle? At the end of the process, did you feel that you were back where you started, or was there a sense of spiraling upward toward greater knowledge and more effective involvements?

4. How would you summarize the proper relationship between universal principles (such as we find in the documents of Vatican social teaching) and local applications (as when smaller groups use the pastoral circle)? Are the more universal statements merely good background resources for one or two stages of local decision making, or should we think of them as basic starting points?

Chapter 5

Nine Key Themes of Catholic Social Teaching

In the previous four chapters, we examined many important questions that help us understand the significance and background of Catholic social teaching. Because of the great distance we have already traveled, we are now acquainted with the reasons for social action on the part of the Christian community, the historical development of the Church's social teaching, and the scriptural and theological sources of the documents that explain that teaching. In fact, it seems that we have accomplished almost everything except what many readers probably most desire: a detailed exploration of the content of that teaching we have heard so much about.

It is time to reward your patience. This chapter is the "pay-off" as we investigate the actual messages contained in the encyclicals. Recall that the final columns of Table 1 provide a brief statement regarding the challenges and new messages of each of the twelve Vatican social teaching documents. This chapter offers a greatly expanded study of the central topics and arguments of these documents. Instead of marching through the encyclicals in chronological order, we will treat nine themes that form the heart of Catholic social teaching as it has developed over the course of its one-hundred-year tradition.

There is nothing magical about the number nine in this context, and nothing definitive about this particular listing of themes. Similar lists of various length have been compiled by other observers (for examples, see the first three items listed under chapter 5 in the "For Further Study" section). Although these lists rarely match perfectly, there is general agreement about the basic items that belong on a list of the core Catholic social teaching principles. Table 2 (see page 167) offers a listing of these nine themes along with several of the most important texts in the documents of Catholic social teaching that treat each theme.

1. The Dignity of Every Person and Human Rights

The claim that people have great worth and dignity is certainly familiar. In fact, it would be hard to think of a culture or religion that did not in some way affirm the value of human life. But the Catholic Church addresses the topic of human dignity in a special way that leads to some particularly firm conclusions about what is permissible both in individual moral choices and in ethical practices of entire societies. The positions staked out by Catholic social teaching on a wide range of issues is firmly embedded in a complete view of the origin, nature, and destiny of all people.

One key foundation of this picture of human life is that all humans are made in the image and likeness of God. This idea is found in the story of creation that comes to us from the opening chapters of the Book of Genesis. Because we all somehow reflect the image of God in our rational minds and in our physical bodies, we are all entitled to be treated with respect and dignity. Because we are intelligent and free beings, God intends us to be immune from all slavery, manipulation, or exploitation. At all stages of our lives—from the moment of conception through the vulnerable years of childhood and old age to the very moment of natural death—we deserve the care and attention that belong to beings of inestimable worth.

This insistence on the sanctity and infinite value of each human life has led the Catholic Church to uncompromising opposition to various threats to human dignity, including abortion, euthanasia, and capital punishment. In its moral teachings, the Church has courageously held fast to a pro-life position on numerous controversial issues, advocating respect for all human life especially that of the vulnerable and outcast. Perhaps the most articulate spokesman on these matters among American Catholics was the late Cardinal Joseph Bernardin of Chicago. He wrote and spoke frequently about the topic of "a consistent ethic of life." In advocating an attitude of profound respect for the sanctity of life at every moment of its duration, from conception to natural death, Cardinal Bernardin often used the biblical metaphor of the "seamless garment." This comparison suggests that any attack against innocent life is an offense and potential threat to all human life.

One important aspect of human dignity is the notion of *equality*. The Catholic tradition interprets the key moments of the drama of human life in a way that treats all people equally. From God's original bestowal of life (in the act of creation) to the sending of God's Son into the world to save us from sin (in the Incarnation) to the expectation of a final invitation into God's kingdom (in the Resurrection of the Dead), we recognize a fundamental equality in God's gracious activity. Of course, human social life has always been filled with many types of inequalities. When Catholic social teaching calls for a more equal sharing of political power, social status, and economic resources, it is merely extending the Christian doctrine of equal human dignity to the concrete realm of social existence. There are certain things that all children of God deserve, and when vast inequalities prevent people from attaining what they need to preserve their lives and develop their potential, people of faith must speak out against these injustices.

The twentieth century witnessed a remarkable movement toward a worldwide consensus regarding human rights. International covenants (such as the Universal Declaration of Human Rights approved by the United Nations General Assembly in 1948) often base their arguments on the concept of human rights. Beginning especially with *Pacem in Terris* in 1963, the documents of Catholic social teaching also use the language of human rights as one way of expressing what is owed to all human beings by virtue of their dignity. Pope John XXIII dedicated *Pacem in Terris* to a full listing of the many types of human rights, calling these rights "universal, inviolable, and inalienable." Because it was the first strong statement of a human rights position from the Church, this encyclical earned the nickname the "Catholic charter of human rights." The convergence of worldwide opinion, both religious and secular in nature, around human rights is an encouraging sign for the prospect of greater cooperation and further improvement in the social conditions facing people of all nations and creeds.

But it is helpful to note that the Catholic view of human rights is distinctive because it is grounded on a complete theological framework, in which God is the ultimate source of our rights. The Catholic tradition of reflection on human rights is also special in that it always locates rights within human communities. In comparison, purely secular doctrines of rights have no similar foundation in a compelling portrayal of human nature and its origin. In a sense, they are doctrines without a solid theory behind them. They are exposed to the weighty charge that rights just seem to "float around," sticking to people without any justification behind their passing claims.

While secular rights theories are certainly useful in speaking boldly about our immunity from being harmed by others, the claims they make have the shortcoming of not fitting into a shared comprehensive view of the universe. Because they remain quite "thin," such theories can offer little guidance on difficult questions such as how to resolve seemingly interminable conflicts of rights. The treatment of rights in Catholic social teaching reflects most of these same positive concerns and goals, but has the additional advantage of situating "rights talk" within a more satisfying and complete picture of the world. Because it is grounded in reverence for the sanctity of creation and its Creator, the Catholic approach to human rights can consider the entire web of relationships that connect God, the natural environment, persons, governments, and local communities.

2. Solidarity, Common Good, and Participation

This second item on our list serves as an important counterbalance to the first, and helps to prevent a rampant and destructive individualism. Rights should always be placed in the context of solidarity and concern for the well-being of the wider community. If we considered only the dignity and infinite worth of the individual in isolation, we might forget that *rights* come paired with *duties*. All the things that persons have rightful claims to are necessarily matched with the things these same persons are expected to give back to others who depend upon them. The Catholic social encyclicals teach that to be human is to experience not only rights but also obligations to others.

Solidarity is a single word that captures a complex of meanings. It calls attention to the simple and easily observable fact that people are interdependent; they rely upon each other for almost all their biological and social needs. The complex fabric of social life, including human achievements such as language, art, culture, and education, testifies to the many ways we depend on shared efforts in all fields of human endeavors. Using the term "solidarity" means that we recognize human interdependence not only as a necessary fact but also as a positive value in our lives. We cannot realize our full potential or appreciate the full meaning of our dignity unless we share our lives with others and cooperate on projects that hold the promise of mutual benefit.

In his three social encyclicals, that is *Laborem Exercens* ("On Human Work"), *Sollicitudo rei Socialis*, and *Centesimus Annus*, Pope John Paul II repeatedly calls solidarity an essential virtue of social life. He argues that God not only allows us to depend upon each other but absolutely wills us to share ourselves in the context of intimate as well as larger groupings of our neighbors. To be human is to be a social being, one whose very life is and should be bound up with those around us.

Solidarity begins as an inner attitude and, when it has fully taken root within us, expresses itself through numerous external activities that demonstrate our commitment to the well-being of others. Just as children naturally reach out to their peers to build friendships, all humans have a natural propensity to form and nourish many social relationships. Catholic social teaching portrays each person as naturally fitting into the larger society. Except in unusual situations, such as being shipwrecked on a deserted island, human flourishing is always communal and social. The full features of our human nature and dignity come to maturity only in the context of community life, where many relationships develop and ripen.

Two especially important aspects of social life are summarized by a pair of terms frequently linked together in Catholic social teaching: *common good* and *participation*. To speak of the common good is to recognize that there are numerous rightful goals in life beyond our own private benefits. In *Mater et Magistra*, Pope John XXIII defines the common good as "the sum total of those conditions of social living whereby men are enabled more fully and more readily to achieve their own perfection" (no. 65). We all have an obligation to promote the common good by making whatever contributions are necessary to improve the lives of others.

Consider one example that illustrates the obligation of all of us to promote the common good. One of the key conditions for human flourishing in society is the education and maturation of youth. Since this is often an expensive task, and since all of us ultimately have a stake in quality schools, it falls on every member of society to support education. We might imagine an elderly childless couple launching an argument to explain why they should not pay taxes to support education for future generations. Perhaps this couple would base their claims on the argument that they themselves will not benefit from costly improvements in public schools. At first blush, based solely on the logic of self-interest, such an argument seems to make a certain amount of sense. However, an understanding of common good that is consistent with Catholic social teaching would point to the obligation and necessity of all of us, however indirect our stake, to make significant sacrifices for such improvements that will bring broad benefits to society, including future generations.

The other related term is *participation*. As the tradition of Catholic social teaching has unfolded in its full appreciation of the equality of all members of society, the theme of equal participation has come to play a more and more important role in its documents. Each of us has at once a right and a duty to participate in the full range of activities and institutions of social life. To be excluded from playing a significant role in the life of society is a serious injustice, for it frustrates our legitimate aspirations to express our human freedom. Anything that blocks full political participation (such as unreasonable restrictions on voting rights for minorities) or economic participation (such as racial or gender discrimination in education or employment) counts as a serious offense against human rights. A sincere regard for the common good will inspire concerned members of society to oppose such injustices and encourage full participation for all, regardless of differences of race, gender, or creed.

The ordinary way that people participate in the *economy* is through their labor. We will look at Catholic social teaching on questions of work and employment when we examine item six on our list of nine themes. The ordinary way for people to participate in the *political life* of society is through democratic activity that allows them to determine and influence the structures of government. When it is fulfilling its proper role, government is the instrument of a people, not something that drains their resources or threatens to control them. Government is legitimate when it assists our efforts to pursue a happy, prosperous and meaningful life without undue interference with our God-given liberties, including freedom of religion and conscience.

Catholic social teaching portrays government as the privileged agent of the common good and as a natural part of a well-ordered human community. The God who intends people to live together in society also enlightens our minds as we seek to organize our large-scale social cooperation. We naturally turn to the assistance of properly selected public authorities whose policies supplement our private efforts to order society justly. These government officials are entrusted with the task of safeguarding our rights and carrying out our duties to other members of society. Without government as an expression of our solidarity, we could do little to insure peace and advance the cause of social justice.

3. Family Life

Since solidarity is about our most basic sense of belonging to society, then we move next to the most basic unit of society to which we all belong in some way: the family. The family occupies a special place in Catholic social teaching; it is the most intimate sphere in which people cooperate and the first place where children learn about themselves, their individual identities, and their vocations within the wider society.

Church documents sometimes refer to the family as the "domestic church" because it is also where young people first encounter God, form their consciences, and learn moral virtues. Elsewhere it is referred to as the "first cell of society," for no institution can substitute for the important social roles played by families. The responses of justice and charity that are called for in the social encyclicals depend upon decisions made along with our loved ones in the context of family life and on the level of the individual household.

The well-being of the entire society absolutely depends upon healthy families, committed marriages, and responsible parenthood. Family life is where we learn and practice the virtues of love and compassion that allow us to imagine alternatives to the ruthless competition and selfish individualism that we witness all too often in the business world and in our market-based society. Outside of family life, it is rare to witness a spirit of profound self-sacrifice and generous giving to others that does not count the cost to oneself. But within our families, we are not surprised by (and indeed almost expect) repeated acts of forgiveness and self-emptying love on the part of marital partners, parents, and their children. In a world of bewildering complexity and rapid, unpredictable change, the stable relationships of family and home life are like a safe port in a fierce storm. Families are the place where the unconditional love of God is reflected in everyday human activities, where we gain a glimpse of the unity and communion that we hope to find in the Kingdom of God.

But we must also be on guard against excessive idealism about family life. Real-life families experience serious challenges and numerous problems, from within (stemming from their members, who are rarely saints) and from outside (stemming from the world beyond the household). To its credit, *Gaudium et Spes*, the 1965 Vatican II document that contains the most extended treatment of family life of any of the twelve Vatican social teaching documents, describes several of these challenges in a frank and eye-opening way. Several pages of this document are devoted to the problems encountered by families today. *Gaudium et Spes* introduces its survey of these problems with the compassionate observation that:

> . . . serious disturbances are caused in families by modern economic conditions, by influences at once social and psychological, and by the demands of civil society (no. 47).

Many of these problems come from perennial sources of hardship, such as poverty, illness, inattentiveness of family members, materialism, and irresponsibility. Others come from newer pressures, such as overwork, modern rootlessness, the entry of more women into the workforce with resulting scarcity of reliable daycare, and the adjustments associated with divorce and blended families. Indeed, our thinking about family life itself is constantly challenged by the existence of new family patterns that do not conform to our accustomed notions of the nuclear family. Unlike in years past, households form and combine for nontraditional reasons and with new relationships between children and adults drawn from several generations.

On many of these items, wise public policies, such as social welfare programs, subsidized provision of quality daycare, medical leave, unemployment compensation, and retirement benefits can make a huge contribution to the health of millions of families. Pope John Paul II offers a comprehensive list of constructive government policies toward families in his 1981 encyclical *Laborem Exercens.* Some nations, particularly in Western Europe, are far ahead of the United States in adopting such family-friendly economic policies. Catholic social teaching suggests that any compassionate society will count the health of family life as among the highest priorities on its policy agenda.

4. Subsidiarity and the Proper Role of Government

Of these nine items, this one has the title that will probably baffle the most people. The term *subsidiarity* comes from the Latin word for "assistance," and it refers to the way the various levels of society should relate to each and assist one another in bringing about the best outcomes for all people. The term was coined by Pope Pius XI who, in the 1931 encyclical *Quadragesimo Anno*, draws a distinction between "higher collectivities" on the one hand and "lesser and subordinate bodies" on the other hand.

The Pope's message is about the proper division of labor among human institutions. For example, there are some tasks and goals that should be accomplished on the local level, and others that are more appropriate for larger entities such as national governments. While it is not always immediately clear which level applies best to a given task, the rule of thumb laid out in Catholic social teaching is to rely as much as possible on those solutions that are closest to the people affected and which employ the smallest groupings and mechanisms that are still effective. Abraham Lincoln was thinking of the same delicate balance when he stated:

> The legitimate object of government is to do for a community of people whatever they need to have done, but cannot do at all or cannot as well do, for themselves—in their separate and individual capacities.

This wise description of the proper balance to be struck in relying on government action is a better guide to real-life situations than the often quoted but simplistic motto, "he governs best who governs least."

One of the benefits of the principle of subsidiarity is that it respects the natural groupings that people form with their neighbors. For example, if the people of a small village agree on a goal (say, building a road or cleaning up a polluted swamp) and have the means to accomplish it, they should avoid involving any larger bodies in the task. Pope Pius XI specifically mentions not only geographical but also vocational groupings (trade and professional bodies such as labor unions and the medieval occupational guilds they replaced) among those human associations that should exercise rightful autonomy where possible. Their activities should not be subsumed under larger umbrellas unless there is good reason and some real benefits from this shift.

But Pius XI hastens to add an insight that our common sense also suggests: there are many occasions when larger bodies can make a real and indispensable contribution to local efforts. In terms of American government, we would speak here of the need for state or even federal assistance to supplement the efforts of municipalities and counties. In many projects, such as public works, building roads, infrastructure improvements, pollution control, and even police investigations, there is no substitute for government activity on higher levels.

As many moments in human history demonstrate, large-scale efforts of national governments are often the only effective means of marshaling the resources needed for immense and complex tasks. Without the authority and funding mechanisms of a centralized government, neither national defense nor a parks system nor many other desirable items would be possible. This insight is captured in the common expression, "you should have *only* the government you need, but also *all* the government you need." While it will always be necessary to make judgments on a case-by-case basis, a good summary of the wisdom of subsidiarity is, "as small as possible, but big when necessary."

Pope Pius XI lived in an age that was witnessing the growth of totalitarianism, including the threat of fascism as well as communism. His message to resist needless centralization echoes to our own day, when so many people also recognize the drawbacks and inefficiencies of an overreliance on large-scale government. It is certainly desirable to respect the authority of local institutions, from voluntary associations to families themselves. Nevertheless, we must remember that national governments are not to be portrayed as our enemies but, rather, as the very instruments by which we join our efforts together when necessary to accomplish important goals that could not be addressed on local levels.

As long as our society maintains a robust set of medium-sized bodies and voluntary associations that bridge the levels between individuals and their national government, a healthy balance can be established that averts the threat of totalitarian control. People will still have the freedom to join clubs and participate in local affairs without feeling dwarfed by "big brother," that is, an overactive and intrusive government. Most citizens will discover their richest satisfactions in belonging to not just a nation but also to organizations of like-minded people in groups such as the Knights of Columbus, Rotary, Elks Clubs, the St. Vincent de Paul Society, and numerous leisure associations, from bowling leagues to golf clubs. Through these affiliations, society can progress smoothly, taking advantage of the efficiency of large-scale endeavors at the same time as it respects the rights and prerogatives of individuals and local bodies.

At the heart of the principle of subsidiarity, then, is the distinction between state and society. Catholic social teaching is always mindful that the strength and vitality of a people goes far beyond its government structures and officials. However useful and necessary government action is, we must never forget that the state is just one small part of the larger society that it is meant to serve, never to control.

5. Property Ownership in Modern Society: Rights and Responsibilities

In chapter four, we took a look at the wise way in which St. Thomas Aquinas treated the difficult subject of private property. He recognized two competing values: the common good, and the individual ownership of property. As we saw earlier in this chapter, a true respect for the common good suggests that the material things necessary for a good life should be widely available for use by the whole human community. But the Catholic tradition also makes us aware of the benefits of individual ownership, which not only encourage the most efficient and the most orderly of property arrangements but also gives us an incentive to be productive and to care for the goods God has created.

Catholic social teaching has followed the path mapped out by Aquinas regarding property and has attempted to apply his principles to new situations in the modern world. From *Rerum Novarum* on, it has consistently defended the basic right to private ownership of property. But it has also adjusted its message to account for new situations and needs that place prudent limits on property holding and unlimited acquisition of goods. To ignore the needs of our less-fortunate neighbors, whether out of selfish motives or mere neglect, is to frustrate the very purpose of God in creating the material world we share. The Creator intends the common gift of the earth to be used for the nourishment and sustenance of all God's children, not just for the benefit of a few privileged members of society.

A good example of this type of limitation on the holding of property appears in the 1967 encyclical *Popolorum Progressio*. In paragraph 23 of that document, Pope Paul VI reminds us that:

> . . . private property does not constitute for anyone an absolute and unconditional right. No one is justified in keeping for his [or her] exclusive use what he [or she] does not need, when others lack necessities.

In the very next paragraph, the Pope indicates the contemporary injustice that prompted him to repeat this long-held

Christian prohibition against the hoarding of wealth. Those who hold a great deal of property (Paul VI was probably thinking about the wealthy owners of Latin American *latifundia*, or landed estates) hurt the poor when they allow their plantations to lie fallow for long periods of time while nearby landowners are close to starvation. The encyclical reaches the judgment that if these tracts of land are "extensive, unused or poorly used" and if these ownership patterns "bring hardship to peoples or are detrimental to the interests of the country, the common good sometimes demands their expropriation."

To *expropriate* property means to take it from its present owner, a course of action not normally recommended in the documents of Catholic social teaching. The earliest social encyclicals strenuously opposed any attempts to seize property, especially socialist and communist programs of nationalization of industry and agricultural lands. According to *Rerum Novarum* (1891) and *Quadragesimo Anno* (1931), this form of socialism was against the natural law and an injustice to all property holders. But by the 1960s, social conditions had changed so much that several recent popes have modified the teaching to reflect new challenges. Even before Pope Paul VI's 1967 argument that some expropriation might be justified in extreme conditions, Pope John XXIII had discussed the need to consider more property as the common possession of the people of a nation. He presented these arguments in paragraphs 51–67 of his 1961 social encyclical *Mater et Magistra*. Let us look at what he says in this passage.

Pope John spends many paragraphs of *Mater et Magistra* surveying recent global developments, such as vast improvements in technology, transportation, and communication. He notes:

> One of the principle characteristics of our time is the multiplication of social relationships, that is, a daily more complex interdependence of citizens. . . . These developments in social living are at once both a symptom and a cause of the growing intervention of public authorities in matters. . . .

Our understanding of property must also adjust to these changed circumstances. Because all people are increasingly dependent upon certain types of industrial production (such as electricity, oil, and communications), the companies that make up these industries must be more responsive to the needs of all people.

John XXIII calls this process of guaranteeing greater accountability and social responsibility "socialization," and he identifies government as its primary agent. Alongside the familiar private obligation upon each of us to pursue the common good, the Church had now come to recognize the legitimacy of public and governmental efforts to exercise socially responsible use of property. By no means does this suggest that all property should be collectivized or that all industries should be nationalized. Rather, it implies that the social character of property can be safeguarded when certain key utilities are regulated or perhaps even owned by the entire people, represented by their government. To us today, this is not really such an unfamiliar idea; many utilities, even in the United States, are considered to be in the public domain or are at least regulated by various government agencies to prevent harmful monopolistic behavior by private corporations.

The notion of socialization was widely misunderstood when *Mater et Magistra* first appeared. Some people, for example, confused it with "socialism." William F. Buckley, a prominent Catholic intellectual and political correspondent, commented: *"Mater si, Magistra no."* With this Latin phrase, he meant that he would continue to consider the Church his spiritual "mother" but no longer a reliable "teacher" on social issues. Buckley and other free-market conservatives feared that John XXIII was advocating not only the prudent limitation of private ownership of property, but its utter elimination. They did not trust the principle of subsidiarity to guard against the rampant centralization of the functions of government. Nor did they welcome the Vatican II document *Gaudium et Spes* which, four years later in 1965, reaffirmed socialization as an important principle to advance the common good and the rights of the most vulnerable members of modern interdependent societies.

We have already seen Pope Paul VI's treatment in 1967 of the occasional necessity of expropriation of private property. Twenty years after that comment in *Popolorum Progressio*, Pope John Paul II introduced yet another way of thinking about limitations upon private property. In paragraph 42 of *Sollicitudo rei Socialis*, he wrote:

> . . . the goods of this world are equally meant for all.
> The right to private property is valid and necessary,
> but it does not nullify the value of this principle.
> Private property, in fact, is under a social mortgage.

Anyone who has ever held a mortgage on a house surely knows what this means. Just as we cannot truthfully say that we own a house until the mortgage is completely paid off, we cannot really say that we are the final owners of the material gifts that come from God. As long as we remain God's handiwork, our holding of property is strictly conditioned on fulfilling our social obligations to the rest of God's creatures. To see our property as coming under a "social mortgage" means that we cannot disregard the needs of the less fortunate, use our property in ways that harm them, or exclude them from full participation in society. John Paul II's words, like those of several of his predecessors who issued social encyclicals, give us much to think about regarding the social dimension of the property we hold.

6. The Dignity of Work, Rights of Workers, and Support for Labor Unions

As we saw in chapter three, the historical origin of the tradition of Catholic social teaching is bound up with the Church's concern for workers. Social Catholicism in the nineteenth century was dedicated to improving the conditions of labor wherever possible. In many ways, the Church was ahead of its time in advocating for better treatment of workers. Today we take for granted many of the original goals of these early church efforts. Government has become the instrument that now enforces prevailing labor protections, at least in most industrialized nations. These include minimum wage laws, safety and health regulations, pension plans, social insurance, and the rights of workers to organize into labor unions.

The two encyclicals with the most extensive treatment of labor issues are *Rerum Novarum* in 1891 and *Laborem Exercens* in 1981. Although separated by ninety years, they share at least one remarkable feature in common: both show a tendency to move back and forth rather quickly between the worlds of abstract theological reflection and practical principles of worker justice. This "quick passage" from eternal truths to specific measures reflects the great confidence shared by both their authors that the nitty-gritty reforms advocated in these documents are fully congruent with the will of God for the world. Both Leo XIII and John Paul II hold up an ideal of worker justice that demands close attention to the concrete conditions that face workers in the actual workplace and in the labor markets that determine the availability of work and the terms of their employment. While both popes respect the fact that the great diversity of conditions complicates the way broad principles of worker justice are applied from place to place, neither is afraid to insist on the importance of concrete measures, such as "living wages" and reasonable work hours, for the entire workforce.

Perhaps the most controversial of the positions regarding work staked out within Catholic social teaching concerns the Church's support for labor unions. Workers' rights to organize and enter into collective bargaining are considered an important outgrowth of other human rights, such as the right to free association and the right to participate fully in the economic and political life of society. Of course, we all know that labor unions have often been criticized on a number of grounds, sometimes with good reason. For example, we often hear them associated with corruption, favoritism, and the threat of disruptive and potentially violent strikes. They also are accused of driving up the cost of doing business and sacrificing the international competitiveness of domestic industries because of the allegedly excessive wage demands they make.

Clearly, there are some problematic aspects of union activity. Yet Catholic social teaching contends that a world without labor unions would witness a much less favorable environment for achieving justice and an equitable sharing of the earth's resources. Without the ability to combine their voices through organized labor, workers would be at the mercy of their far more powerful employers who might take advantage of their inferior position. Labor unions are crucial elements in the overall balance of power in the economy, and Catholic social teaching consistently portrays them as playing a constructive role in the pursuit of economic justice. Indeed, it is increasingly a source of concern that in many places unions seem to be on the decline. As unions represent a smaller and smaller percentage of the overall workforce and enjoy a lower profile in our economic life, the power of workers to bargain effectively to protect their rights will unfortunately diminish greatly.

Alongside its support of labor unions, Catholic social teaching contains many additional messages about work. Here labor is portrayed as neither a necessary evil nor merely a means to the end of supporting family life; rather, labor is presented as something that is intrinsically good for us. In our work, we can discover rich meaning and develop our potential. Even in the humdrum routine of daily life in the workplace, work is more than a taxing or boring necessity. Engaging in labor opens up new avenues of communication and planning with our colleagues, with whom we toil for common purposes and build up mutual respect. Work represents an opportunity to collaborate with others and to contribute our special talents to the wider society.

Besides its practical benefits, human labor also includes theological significance, as it contains our response to the God who invites us to become co-creators of the material world. This is why human work should never be treated as a mere commodity, something to be bought and sold in a cavalier way, in impersonal markets. This is also why workers must not be treated as just another cog in the huge machine of production, an attitude that offends the dignity of all. These concerns are especially prominent in *Laborem Exercens*, where John Paul II repeatedly insists on the "priority of labor over capital." Through labor, we pursue not only a job or a career, but a vocation—a calling in which we are summoned by God to develop our capabilities and to follow the Carpenter from Nazareth on our path of discipleship. Catholic social teaching is a great resource for future efforts to develop a full-blown *theology of work* and indeed to discover a *spirituality of labor* appropriate for our age.

7. Colonialism and Economic Development

A major topic of Catholic social teaching in the last half-century concerns the legacy of colonialism and the challenge of economic development in the poorest parts of the world. Everyone agrees that there are large and disturbing gaps between the world's richest and poorest lands. Most people further agree that the history of European colonialism and superpower imperialism have played an important role in causing these glaring disparities. The remaining differences of opinion concern the specific assignment of blame and the hard task of choosing the wisest strategy to address global poverty and underdevelopment today.

Catholic social teaching weighs in on these complicated topics by offering two sets of ideas. The *first* is the more consistent part of its message. The Church repeatedly reminds us that we all have a moral obligation to care deeply about world poverty and to do all we can to address this scourge against our common humanity. Despite the artificial divisions of people into races, religions, and nations, we are all part of one human family. Hunger and disease in any part of the world should be a concern for all of us and should demand our urgent attention. The strenuous efforts of people in the richest nations to combat poverty in the poorest lands, even thousands of miles away, are essential expressions of human solidarity.

Repeated calls for "mutual assistance among nations" and "taking into account the interests of others" are sprinkled throughout paragraphs 157–211 of Pope John XXIII's 1961 letter *Mater et Magistra*, the first section of any social encyclical to deal extensively with global poverty. The message that we cannot remain indifferent to any human suffering, no matter how far away it might be, is heard frequently in practically all the social encyclicals since then. If we are indeed to fulfill our role as "our brother's keeper," then we must fight the temptation of selfishness and isolationism, and truly involve ourselves in advancing the well-being of the very poorest residents of our planet. While we often hear the expressions "First World and Third World" or "North and South," we are called to look beyond these artificial divisions to the deeper unity of all those who share the earth.

The *second* way Catholic social teaching addresses poverty and underdevelopment is to invite believers to ponder the causes of these problems and to offer suggestions for improvement. This message is harder to summarize because the advice offered by church leaders has shifted over time. At first the proposals in the encyclicals remained cautious and halfhearted, as they focused mainly on the level of urging individual moral enlightenment and recommending the practice of virtues such as charity and prudence. This may be quite understandable, since it is much easier to call attention to problems such as world poverty than it is to enter the controversial arena of debate over the precise causes and most effective solutions to these problems. But as the seriousness of global poverty became clearer, the Church felt a new urgency to get beyond the level of vague recommendations, such as *Mater et Magistra*'s somewhat timid call for "international cooperation." In a post-colonial age, Catholic social teaching needed to get more specific about the changes that were so desperately needed. The time had come to start asking about specifics: What kind of cooperation? To fight which evils? To change which structures?

Among the church leaders most impatient for sweeping changes were the bishops assembled at the Second Vatican Council, including Pope Paul VI, who presided over the end of the Council and led the Church until 1978. Because the bishops at Vatican II were assembled from all over the world and shared close quarters for many months, they had ample opportunity to consult with one another. They talked frequently about the dire condition facing millions, and compared notes about how their efforts to be good pastors were so often frustrated by the desperate poverty that discouraged, disrupted, and even claimed millions of lives in their various homelands.

Several inspiring passages in *Gaudium et Spes* reflect the concern and sincere search for solutions on the part of the world's bishops. An especially stirring section, paragraphs 63 to 72, includes a lament over the state of a world in which, all too often, "luxury and misery rub shoulders." Paul VI, the first pope to travel widely outside of Europe, went even further in addressing the Church's concerns about maldistribution. He dedicated major sections of three important social teaching documents (*Popolorum Progressio, Octogesima Adveniens,* and *Evangelii Nuntiandi*) to the problem of world poverty. Here and in many other writings and speeches, Pope Paul sincerely wrestled with the urgent puzzle of what should be done by the Church, by individual nations, and by international agencies to address global underdevelopment.

The writings of Paul VI ushered the Catholic Church into a new era of reflection and advocacy regarding international economics. After the 1967 encyclical *Popolorum Progressio*, there was no turning back to the former timid approach that consisted mostly of hand-wringing and moralizing about how the wealthy should find it in their hearts to offer charitable assistance to the destitute. The Pope boldly identified the vast inequalities between rich and poor as unjust results of sinful structures of world trade and finance that shut the majority of the world's population out of opportunities for self-improvement. While some of the blame might be placed on past generations and the inheritance of European colonialism from previous centuries, the continuation of these imbalances must be confronted and condemned.

Pope Paul VI contended that economies must be restructured to serve true human needs, not the wants of the most affluent. He advocated such measures as: 1) land reform in the Third World; 2) an end to export-maximizing policies that warped local economies by favoring the production of goods that would be most profitable for a few, not most useful for the many; and 3) more generous international aid to support micro-development and to increase the availability of credit to farmers and townspeople in Africa, Asia, and Latin

America. Measures such as these are designed to place more of the tools required for self-improvement in the hands of those who currently have no access to these critical resources.

Sometimes in our reflection on development issues, the word *tools* is used metaphorically, standing for educational and employment opportunities. In other instances, we are talking about tools in the literal sense. Micro-development projects that supply sewing machines to women's cooperatives in Africa or farm implements to villagers in Central America are the practical forms of assistance that produce tangible results to improve the lives of the most vulnerable. Often what is required is not necessarily an outright gift but, rather, access to credit and marketing arrangements that make possible modest income-generating activities such as handcrafts and fish farming. To its credit, the Church has sponsored numerous projects such as these through Catholic Relief Services, Caritas International, and similar faith-based organizations, but far more needs to be done through international agencies, religious and secular alike. If global solidarity is to have real meaning beyond pleasant-sounding phrases, then Christians and all others must commit themselves to these concrete measures to restructure the world economy, even where these measures may entail sacrifices on the part of the rich.

The path taken by Paul VI was continued by John Paul II, whose three social encyclicals also emphasize the structural dimensions of global injustice and maldistribution of resources. Especially in his 1987 encyclical *Sollicitudo rei Socialis*, John Paul bemoans the growing gap between rich and poor nations, frequently contrasting the superabundance enjoyed by a few with the desperate struggle for survival experienced by so many. He condemns the excesses of wasteful consumerism and materialism as evidence of a distortion he calls "super-development."

Elsewhere in *Sollicitudo rei Socialis*, the Pope identifies a number of "structures of evil," including the crushing burden of international debt, the arms race, and a form of economic domination often termed "neo-colonialism." John Paul II denounces these harmful trends and patterns which are responsible for the worsening plight of the poorest as they suffer from the effects of unemployment, a housing crisis, illiteracy, and other obstacles to their full human development. In prophetic words in paragraph 37 of that encyclical, John Paul attributes many of these global problems to two basic social sins: the "all-consuming desire for profit" and the "thirst for power." These evils have come to resemble idolatries in the modern world. We will examine the notion of "social sin" or "structures of evil" more fully in chapter seven.

It may be hard for average Christians to know how to respond to the Church's challenging message about worldwide economic development. Most middle-class churchgoers in the affluent nations may have a vague sense of guilt about living in a society that somehow benefits from the cheap labor and resources extracted from Third World nations, but they probably have few ideas of how to go about making improvements. After all, when Paul VI called for a "civilization of love" or John Paul II urged a "more authentic development," they had in mind a thorough restructuring of worldwide patterns of trade, production, and finance that would spread the benefits of economic life more widely. Although Catholic social teaching seeks to energize us to attack these problems, the staggering dimensions of the task ahead can easily paralyze us.

Because none of us in isolation has sufficient power to change the large economic and political structures that determine present conditions, our model of change will have to be one of gradual and modest action, each of us pitching in as we are able. But even if our progress is measured in baby steps rather than giant leaps, we cannot ignore the call to all Christians to contribute in some ways to alleviate the suffering of our poorest neighbors here and abroad. Besides being individually generous with the goods we personally control, we are urged by Catholic social teaching to look for new expressions of solidarity with the poor. We might join campaigns for worker justice, boycott products from sweatshops, or pressure Congress and the World Bank to forgive more of the staggering world debt.

These and similar action steps of our own design can be creative ways of responding personally to the general call to global responsibility that comes from the Church. It is understandable, of course, that most of the time our energies and imaginations are focused on the smaller circle of our families, workplaces, and neighborhoods. But we should also take to heart the insightful (if somewhat cliched) bumper-sticker message, to "think globally, act locally."

8. Peace and Disarmament

In the documents of Catholic social teaching, the goal of justice is closely linked to the ideal of peace. The proper ordering of God's creation includes not only prosperity and a fair distribution of resources but also the security and stability that is so well summarized in the Hebrew word for peace: *shalom*. Meaning more than just a temporary absence of open hostilities, the ideal of shalom calls us to a thorough respect for all our neighbors in relationships that are characterized by an ever deeper trust and a commitment to providing mutual assistance.

Of course, history has taught us many hard lessons that lead us to expect anything but the full attainment of the ideals of shalom. Every human age has witnessed wars, civil strife, genocide, and ethnic conflict of greatly disturbing proportions. Our inhumanity to one another has been sparked by greed, hatred, and sometimes even allegedly religious motivations. Christian responses to war and violence must go beyond merely vague feelings of distress and regret to genuine and effective strategies of peacemaking. Of all the possible approaches to the task of building peace, the two dominant Christian approaches to peace are pacifism and the just-war theory.

In chapter four we noted the development of the just-war theory as one Christian response to the conflicting values present in the real world of human sin and division. From the start, Christians rejected the extreme position of the "total war" approach as completely opposed to the teachings of Christ, but after a few centuries questions began to surface about whether some types of "limited warfare" might be allowable. Starting with Augustine, Christian thinkers began to justify the use of force against unjust aggressors in certain circumstances as the most appropriate way to respond to the command to demonstrate love for others with all the means at our disposal.

The Christian presumption against violence gave way to the noble desire to protect the innocent from harm. Many believers reached the conclusion that the best we can do in these difficult situations is to limit the damage while we defend innocent civilians by means of the deadly force we otherwise would choose to avoid. Taking up arms in justified causes such as these came to be referred to as *strange acts of love*, undertaken with the same reluctance that parents feel when they are forced to discipline their unruly children. Because it insists on employing the absolute minimum of force to achieve the objective of resolving conflicts, the just-war theory at its best can never be used as a "fig leaf" to exact disproportionate revenge or to support militarism or extreme nationalism. The just-war theory came to form the mainstream of Christian reflection on violence for many centuries, and the documents of modern Catholic social teaching generally assume this stance in the few places where they treat issues of war and peace in any detail or at any length.

Recall that chapter four's treatment of the just-war theory was intended to illustrate how human reason serves as an important source of Catholic social teaching and Christian ethics in general. The point we were making there was that theologians reasoned their way to the criteria of the just-war theory, rather than finding this approach in any other already existing Christian source. Another of the four sources we examined is revelation, specifically Scripture. When we look at the New Testament, and particularly at the Gospels in their portrayals of the life and teaching of Jesus, we find no obvious support for the just-war theory, or for any approach that would permit the use of force, even to defend innocent lives. Jesus did not lift a finger to save his own life and, in fact, rebuked those who drew the sword to defend him. Many of the sayings of Jesus lend credibility to the pacifists' claim that a true follower of Christ follows a strict policy of nonviolence, never resorting to force for self-defense or even in defense of innocent neighbors.

There are many versions and traditions of pacifism. Some of these are inspired by the New Testament and are practiced by communities of Christians, such as the Mennonites and several other groups which began as off-shoots of the Protestant Reformation. Within modern Catholicism, advocates of pacifism have been rare, but some branches of lay movements, such as the Catholic Worker, have been outspoken in support of a strict nonviolence lifestyle. The issue of who actually qualifies as a pacifist becomes complicated when we start considering distinctions between related schools of thought, such as "nonviolence," "nonresistance," and "passive resistance to evil." Despite the complexity of the topic, suffice it to say that, until quite recently, pacifism seldom received much serious attention in Catholic circles.

We would look in vain through the twelve Vatican social teaching documents for a detailed treatment of the relative merits of pacifism and the just-war theory. The encyclicals generally assume that a proportionate and carefully ordered use of force, when justified by a serious threat to a nation or to innocent people, can qualify as a socially responsible reaction when other options have been exhausted. Several times, popes take the opportunity to decry how regrettable the resort to violence is, urging negotiation as an alternative to counterattacks to aggressors. Although several of the documents use phrases such as "never again war!" the basic stance of the encyclical tradition remains in the just-war camp. However much they hate war, popes have been reluctant to deny states the right they claim to engage in what they consider to be legitimate defense. The principle that warfare might be justified under certain conditions remains dominant in Catholic social thought.

Especially noteworthy is *Pacem in Terris*, the 1963 encyclical written by John XXIII, one of several recent popes who witnessed the horrors of war firsthand. John had served in the Italian army during World War I and was terrified by the prospect of further escalating violence, especially if it were directed against civilians. He wrote *Pacem in Terris* in the wake of the Berlin and Cuban Missile Crises, when the superpower rivalry had recklessly placed the world on the brink of nuclear war. His plea for peaceful resolution of differences is poignant, especially where he dedicates fifteen paragraphs (nn. 109–119 and 126–129) to a description of the merits of disarmament and negotiation. Pope John even quotes the words of his predecessor, Pius XII, the Pope who agonized so long over the bloody course of the Second World War, which swept around his lonely perch in the Vatican: "Nothing is lost by peace; everything may be lost by war."

There are several recent indications that Catholic social teaching is moving toward a position that is somewhat closer to pacifism, as more doubts are cast on how the just-war theory is applied in modern circumstances. Obviously, in a nuclear age, it is hard to imagine how the just-war criteria (which prohibit disproportionate responses and the targeting of civilians) can justify many of the ways current weapons are likely to be used. In light of the ever present threat of quick escalation of hostilities from rifles to tanks to nuclear weapons, we should be hesitant to justify the use of even conventional weapons, especially in tense regions such as the Middle East and the Indian subcontinent. Further, many voices within and beyond the Church have pointed out how often the just-war theory has been misused in cynical efforts to cover up self-interested aggression. Pope John Paul II, in several statements issued during the 1990s (on the occasions of the Persian Gulf War and later air strikes by the United States and its allies against Iraq and in the Balkans), scolded world powers for a premature resort to force before the full range of peaceful channels had been exhausted.

Perhaps the two most significant indications of a more favorable view of pacifist stances within Catholicism came not from recent popes but from gatherings of bishops. First, Vatican II's document *Gaudium et Spes* specifically advocates the rights of conscientious objectors or, as it describes them, "those who for reasons of conscience refuse to bear arms" (no. 79). This novel addition to Catholic social teaching opens the way to seeing this pacifist response to the military draft, at least on the individual level, as a justifiable position worthy of respect. Second, the United States bishops' 1983 pastoral letter "The Challenge of Peace" went to great lengths to explain the pacifist position and treated it more sympathetically than any other major document of the Church. It lifted up the contribution of this minority position in taking seriously the universal call to commit ourselves to peacemaking and to begin this task within our own hearts and through the lifestyle choices we make. By returning to the New Testament and paying close attention to the signs of the times in a dangerous world, Catholic social teaching may be on the brink of passing a further negative judgment on almost all forms of warfare.

If we follow the U.S. bishops' call to take seriously the task of peacemaking, we will soon discover that we are not alone in walking this path of shalom. The Christian tradition contains many rich resources beyond official church teachings that feed our hunger for knowing and pursuing the way of peace. Spiritual writers such as St. Francis of Assisi and social commentators such as Leo Tolstoy offer inspiring words that challenge us to imagine a world of true and lasting harmony. Organized groups such as Pax Christi and Plowshares extend to us opportunities to pursue activism dedicated to building a more peaceful world.

Perhaps the greatest American Catholic witness to peace comes from the Catholic Worker, a lay movement founded in 1933 by Dorothy Day and Peter Maurin. Although best known for publishing a newspaper and sponsoring remarkable houses of hospitality for the needy, members of the Catholic Worker count among their primary goals the building up of a firm witness to peace. The 1987 document "Aims and Means of the Catholic Worker" explains the inspiration and principles of this approach to peacemaking:

> Jesus calls us to fight against violence with the spiritual weapons of prayer, fasting, and noncooperation with evil. Refusal to pay taxes for war, to register for conscription, to comply with any unjust legislation; participation in nonviolent strikes and boycotts, protests or vigils; withdrawal of support for dominant systems, corporate funding, or usurious practices are all excellent means to establish peace.

Even those who are unable to adopt for themselves all aspects of this approach may affirm the utter dedication of the Catholic Worker movement to offer alternatives and shape our lives so that peacemaking becomes one of the central concerns of our everyday lives. We owe a great debt of gratitude to Dorothy Day, Peter Maurin, and their followers for supplying this extraordinary vision for the pursuit of holiness and shalom in the modern world.

9. Option for the Poor and Vulnerable

In one sense, the notion of the "preferential option for the poor" is relatively new to Catholic social teaching, as this phrase appeared in no papal social encyclical until 1987, and in no church documents at all until 1979. But in another sense, the notion of the preferential option for those who are weak and vulnerable has been present within the Christian tradition from the very start. The ministry of Jesus, in both words and deeds, was deeply wrapped up with this commitment to the well-being of the least fortunate. Without using the actual phrase "preferential option," the Church has practiced this option in many ways, formal and informal, as it has placed concern for the most vulnerable members of society among its top priorities.

Echoes of the preferential option for the poor are strong in the stirring opening sentence of the Vatican II document *Gaudium et Spes:*

> The joys and the hopes, the griefs and the anxieties of the [people] of this age, especially those who are poor or in any way afflicted, these too are the joys and hopes, the griefs and anxieties of the followers of Christ (no. 1).

In identifying itself with the concerns of the poor, the Church is here interpreting its entire mission as one of service to those in need. Bringing the gospel to people in the fullest sense means caring simultaneously for their many needs, spiritual and material. The Church is most clearly itself when it is acting on the imperative to meet the urgent needs of the most vulnerable—the ones Jesus Christ so loves.

The worldwide church inherits the actual phrase "preferential option for the poor" from documents of the 1979 meeting of CELAM, the abbreviation for the Spanish words translated as the episcopal conference of Latin America. At that meeting in Puebla, Mexico, as at the previous CELAM meeting in Medellin, Colombia in 1968, the bishops of those lands so sharply divided between extremes of rich and poor boldly identified the Church with the struggles of the poor. This decisive shift was not meant to exclude anyone from the life or concerns of the Church, and certainly was not an invitation to pass judgments upon certain people because their bank accounts were too large.

Rather, the significance of this shift lies in the way it reverses a centuries-long pattern that had warped the proper understanding of the mission of the Church. As long as the Church was perceived as aligned with the wealthy landholders of Latin America, it would remain a hindrance to the full human development of the poor in that region. If the vast majority of people continued to see the Church as a tool in the hands of the upper-class bosses who were indifferent to their well-being, then this perception would prevent the Church from ever becoming the "True Church" of the poor Jesus.

Clearly, the significance of this sudden about-face in the Church's self-understanding was hard to explain outside of Latin America. To observers from other continents where social class divisions were never as sharp, it hardly made sense. The Church is always meant to be an agent of reconciliation between all people, so it may be misleading to think of the Church as "taking sides" in any way at all. The forceful restatement of the Church's mission was only necessary in

Latin America because of the need to correct a long history of clerical abuse and warped priorities.

Vatican social teaching had never gotten off on such a wrong track. From its very beginning, when nineteenth-century European Social Catholicism started to notice and address the plight of hard-pressed working families, this tradition of social concern had consistently expressed the Church's mission to act as Jesus had acted in befriending the poor of his time. In fact, the 1991 encyclical *Centesimus Annus* contains a passage in which Pope John Paul II interprets *Rerum Novarum*'s call, a full century earlier, to improve the conditions of workers as a manifestation of the "preferential option for the poor" long before the phrase was coined. John Paul points to the similarity between the Church's role as advocate of the poor in 1891 and 1991 as evidence of the "church's constant concern for and dedication to categories of people who are especially beloved to the Lord Jesus" (no. 11).

The entire tradition of Catholic social teaching, including all nine themes we have surveyed in this chapter, can be interpreted as a unified effort on the part of church leaders to encourage a more humane society where the most vulnerable members are better protected from harm. With its limited financial resources, the Church itself can do only so much to advance the lives of the poor. However, popes and bishops, as the official voices of the Church, have exerted great efforts to speak publicly about political, economic, and social issues that have profound impact upon the prospects of our neediest neighbors. The rationale for all the Church's efforts in this regard may be summarized precisely as the desire to make a preferential option for the poor.

If these church efforts really do bear fruit, then what would the results look like? If the message of justice and peace within Catholic social teaching takes root in the hearts of many believers, these people would work energetically for a better world, a world characterized by not only acts of individual *charity* but also structures of *justice* and equity for all people. Discrimination and unfair barriers to progress would be eliminated. True human development would be fostered by wider access to property and socially responsible policies of businesses and governments throughout the world. We would measure all our institutions, from schools to corporations to social clubs, by how they treat all members of society, especially the poorest. Priorities would be altered so that more of the benefits of our richly blessed world would find their way toward those who currently possess the least. In a prosperous age like ours, no one should be excluded from a fair set of opportunities or experience the disturbing fear of permanent powerlessness.

Catholic social teaching includes a call for involvement in collaborative efforts to invite all people into the social mainstream; it is not an ethic for lazy or complacent people. To adopt the principles of Catholic social thought is to agree that we all need to work hard so that full participation is extended to all, without favoritism or discrimination. We all have something to contribute to the common good, and all may benefit from the gifts that we bring to the common table of human community and solidarity.

Questions for Reflection

1. Which of these nine themes of Catholic social teaching do you consider most important? Are certain ones more foundational than others, which build upon the more basic ones?

2. How would you explain the principle of subsidiarity to a child, using the simplest possible language? Do you think that this technical-sounding idea is at root a "common-sense" principle that almost anyone can understand if it is explained properly?

3. How good are the tools given to us by recent Catholic social teaching on private property? Do you think we strike the proper balance between the individual and social functions of property when we speak of 1) socialization, 2) the "social mortgage on property," and even 3) the possibility of a justified expropriation of some means of production?

4. Besides the positions mentioned in section 6 of this chapter, such as support for organized labor and basic worker rights, what else could the Church be doing to foster a sense of the dignity of all human labor? Can you think of concrete measures for spiritual enrichment, theological education, or outreach programs that would demonstrate greater church commitment to improving the lives of all who work?

5. Many readers might feel that the Church's treatment of families (see section 3 of this chapter) is too sketchy to be of much help. What more should the Church say about family life and the challenges facing all families today?

6. Do you find yourself favoring the approach of the just-war theory or of pacifism? What are the strengths and weaknesses of each of these Christian approaches to the task of peacemaking?

7. Do you see the "preferential option for the poor" as mostly a new element of the Church's social message or mainly as a continuation of what came before? How would you defend your opinion?

Table 2
Key Texts for Nine Themes in Catholic Social Teaching

Theme	Most Important Texts
The Dignity of Every Person and Human Rights	*Pacem in Terris* 8–38 *Gaudium et Spes* 12–19 *Centesimus Annus* 6–11
Solidarity, Common Good, and Participation	*Pacem in Terris* 98–108 *Gaudium et Spes* 26–32, 68–75 *Sollicitudo rei Socialis* 35–40
Family Life	*Gaudium et Spes* 47–52 *Octogesima Adveniens* 13 *Laborem Exercens* 10, 19
Subsidiarity and the Proper Role of Government	*Quadragesimo Anno* 76–87 *Mater et Magistra* 51–77, 122–77 *Pacem in Terris* 140–1
Property Ownership in Modern Society: Rights and Responsibilities	*Quadragesimo Anno* 44–52 *Mater et Magistra* 51–67, 104–21 *Centesimus Annus* 30–43
The Dignity of Work, Rights of Workers, and Support for Labor Unions	*Rerum Novarum* 1–3, 20–1, 31–8 *Mater et Magistra* 68–81 *Laborem Exercens* 1–27
Colonialism and Economic Development	*Mater et Magistra* 157–211 *Pacem in Terris* 121–5 *Popolorum Progressio* 1–87
Peace and Disarmament	*Pacem in Terris* 109–119 *Gaudium et Spes* 77–90 U.S. Bishops' "The Challenge of Peace"
Option for the Poor and Vulnerable	*Gaudium et Spes* 1 *Octogesima Adveniens* 23 *Centesimus Annus* 11

Chapter 6

The Role of Catholic Social Teaching Today

In chapter five, we examined nine of the major themes treated in the documents of Catholic social teaching. Although our survey of themes in that one short chapter (or even in one or two short books) could only scratch the surface of this tradition, we noted a great richness of complexity and detail in these teachings. Many aspects of political and economic life in society are treated in the pages of the encyclicals, which stake out careful positions on the justice dimensions of politics and economics in the modern world.

The task of this chapter is to answer some of the most obvious questions that arise once we have digested the basic content of these teachings about faith, peace, and justice: How can we go about the task of applying the messages of Catholic social teaching? Should we interpret it as supporting some already existing economic system, or is it equally critical of all current alternatives, such as capitalism and socialism? Is it a complete blueprint for an ideal society, or are its challenges more of a modest scatter-shot attempt to address serious injustices? Do the judgments reached by church officials threaten to interfere with the political and economic orders about which bishops and popes clearly lack experience and expertise? What is the purpose of writing and publishing all these documents, anyway?

A Blueprint? An Ideology? A "Third Way"?

Ever since the beginning of the modern tradition of social encyclicals over one hundred years ago, controversy has surrounded the Church's attempt to offer advice about the structure of society. Many observers, including scholars, politicians, and journalists, have criticized the entire endeavor, often claiming that the Church has no business stating positions on secular matters. Several of these church documents contain long sections that address these voices, attempt to answer such objections, and clarify the purpose of Catholic social teaching. In the next few paragraphs, we allow a few of these encyclicals to speak for themselves in defining the legitimate role of Catholic social teaching in the mission of the Church.

One important statement on this topic appears in paragraph 76 of the Vatican II social teaching document *Gaudium et Spes*. Here, the Council summarizes the *twin concerns* expressed by several previous popes in order to set the record straight about the proper role of Catholic social teaching. *First*, we are reminded that the Church's intention in speaking out on social issues is the modest one of offering helpful advice, rather than an overly ambitious one of attempting to replace governments or allying itself with certain political forces in opposition to others. *Gaudium et Spes* asserts:

> The role and competence of the church being what it is, she must in no way be confused with the political community, nor bound to any political system.

In other words, the world of politics has its own legitimate logic and operations, and the Church has no intention of dictating its preferred policies or intruding into areas where it has no particular competence.

A few sentences later, the document speaks about the *second concern*, an anxiety that is really the flip side of the first: the danger that the Church will say too *little* about worldly affairs and thereby surrender part of its own rightful mission of spreading the gospel and assisting people in their attempts to flourish. The words of *Gaudium et Spes* here remind us that the Church:

> . . . has the right to pass moral judgments, even on matters touching the political order, whenever basic personal rights, or the salvation of souls make such judgments necessary.

Without this qualification, readers might conclude that the Church had chosen to withdraw from the world and hold its tongue even when it witnesses grave injustices and abuses in political and economic matters. Much to the contrary, the Catholic Church in the decade of the 1960s was increasingly outspoken about social issues. Church leaders summoned up great courage to challenge the intolerable conditions they discovered when the Church rededicated itself to "reading the signs of the times."

But even after these twin concerns were so clearly addressed, some confusion persisted. Commentators from the right, left, and even the center of the political spectrum repeatedly misunderstood the purpose and proper role of

Catholic social teaching. Sometimes they selected just a few isolated sentences from the encyclicals and twisted the words to support their favorite system, whether capitalist or socialist in nature. Others disputed the Church's right to say anything at all about social issues, insisting on a sharp split between religion and politics. It fell to John Paul II, the Pope who will be remembered for his courageous public stance in support of the Polish labor union Solidarity and its leader Lech Walesa, to issue the most complete clarification of the Church's stance: the encyclical *Sollicitudo rei Socialis*.

Published in 1987, just two years before the fall of the Berlin Wall and the end of the Cold War, *Sollicitudo rei Socialis* contains John Paul's reflections on the Church's contribution to a world of greater peace and justice. Permit me to cite this long quotation from paragraph 41, a key section where the Pope states his hopes and expectations for a constructive type of church advocacy:

> The church does not have technical solutions to offer . . . For the church does not propose economic and political systems or programs, nor does she show preference for one or the other, provided that human dignity is properly respected and promoted. . . . But the church is an "expert in humanity," and this leads her necessarily to extend her religious mission to the

> various fields in which men and women expend their
> efforts in search of the always relative happiness
> which is possible in this world, in line with their dig-
> nity as persons . . . [W]hatever affects the dignity of
> individuals and peoples, such as authentic develop-
> ment, cannot be reduced to a "technical problem" . . .
> This is why the church has something to say today . . .
> about the nature, condition, requirements and aims
> of authentic development, and also about the obsta-
> cles which stand in its way. In doing so the church
> fulfills her mission to evangelize . . . The church's
> social doctrine is not a "third way" between liberal
> capitalism and Marxist collectivism, nor even a possi-
> ble alternative to other solutions less radically
> opposed to one another; rather, it constitutes a cate-
> gory of its own. Nor is it an ideology . . . but belongs
> to the field . . . of moral theology.

This passage is rich in meaning and complexity, but a
few key points stand out and deserve to be underlined. First,
the opening and closing sentences point out the difference
between what we might call the "technical" (relating to
detailed nuts and bolts of policy decisions) and the "moral"
(relating strictly to the level of values in society). We could
think of many examples of technical political and economic

question about which the Church has chosen to remain silent. How many members should represent each state in the Senate? What is the proper rate for sales taxes? Should nations recognize international waters as beginning at two, twelve, or a full two hundred miles off the coast of a country for purposes of fishing and mineral rights?

On the one hand, the Church is unlikely to have much of anything substantial to add to the analysis of secular experts about any of these questions. On the other hand, these and most other public policy questions potentially contain moral dimensions about which the Church has much to say. A bad decision on any of these questions (resulting, for example, in extremely high food taxes that squeeze the poor or election laws that underrepresent regions with more minorities or international laws that unduly punish land-locked countries) could provoke a justified appeal to the lessons of Catholic social teaching. When people notice these moral dimensions, it is helpful to turn to religious voices as partners in a sincere dialogue about ethical aspects of public policy. The social ethics of Christianity and indeed of all the religions of the world can make a truly constructive contribution to the moral and social analysis that informs political and economic decisions.

A second item worth exploring in the above quote from John Paul II regards the ideological competition between capitalism and socialism. When he wrote *Sollicitudo rei Socialis*, this rivalry was still intense, and certain supporters of each side were eager to claim the Catholic Church as an ally against their sworn enemies. Now that the Communist bloc has disintegrated, the controversies of earlier decades appear irrelevant, perhaps even absurd to our ears today, but they still shed helpful light on the proper understanding of Catholic social teaching.

The goal of the Church's statements on social issues has never been to ally the Church with a specific party or ideological movement, whether Marxist Communism or free-market capitalism or welfare-state socialism. In fact, it is easy to find serious criticisms of all these systems and others in the encyclicals. Even though certain of the documents have the appearance of leaning a bit toward one side or another of the political spectrum, it is safe to say that Catholic social teaching never gives its unconditional support or approval to any existing economic system.

How, then, should we think of the role of Catholic social teaching? We should certainly take seriously Pope John Paul II's statement that church teaching is not intended to support any particular ideological system. Nor does it aspire to be an ideology of its own, as if finding a compromise "third way" between communism and capitalism would be the ultimate contribution of this long tradition of reflection on life in society. Instead, this body of teachings must always be considered above all as a religious contribution to human society. From its vantage point of theological principles, Catholic social teaching looks down upon the full spectrum of political and economic options and seeks to measure them according to the Church's distinctive view of what contributes to human flourishing.

The yardstick the Church uses to make these measurements has more to do with human dignity and spiritual values (such as the virtues of solidarity and compassion for the poor) than with material goals (such as greater efficiency and increased consumer choice). For that reason, it has never been easy for politicians, economists, or other strictly secular thinkers to understand fully the principled positions of Catholic social thought. Indeed, at times it infuriates potential political coalition partners to learn that the same bishops, clergy, and lay Catholics who applaud their initiatives on certain measures (such as investment in education or health care reform) wind up staunchly opposing them on others (for example, sterilization for population control, abortion, and protections for the family farm). Because its key loyalties go beyond partisan politics or quantifiable economic goals to include deeper theological principles and human values, Catholic social teaching can never be placed on the same level as Marxist Communism or free-market capitalism, as if it were just another system of ideological thought that competes for dominance and influence.

Recall the nine major themes of Catholic social teaching we examined in chapter five. The items making up that survey suggest a series of important questions that people guided by the Church's social thought might use to evaluate any economic policy or political program. Equipped with this set of concerns, we might ask critical questions such as: Will this proposal advance respect for human dignity? for the rights of workers? Will it result in wider participation, or will it marginalize those who are already poor and vulnerable? Is it likely to foster a more peaceful world, or will it further divide and fragment the relationships of nations as well as the people within them?

How, then, may we summarize the role of Catholic social teaching in the modern world? The best brief answer to this question must stress that it aspires to be neither an ideology, a "third way" compromise between existing ideologies of left or right, nor a comprehensive blueprint for a perfect society. Catholic social teaching at its best makes no attempt to impose any models of how to organize social life. But it is bold enough to propose a core set of values that should guide powerful decision makers, whether they are Catholic or adherents of other faiths or members of no religious community at all. These human values, many of which we saw in chapter five, are key criteria for measuring good decisions and policies. The Church in every land seeks to remain a faithful witness to these values, to model responsible behavior, and to teach all who will listen about the benefits of practicing social justice.

Of course, a national leader, legislator, or corporate executive need not agree with the entire Catholic vision of God, the universe, and humanity's place within the cosmos in order to agree with these core values and criteria. But a picture of human flourishing that includes such principles as human rights, the necessity of peacemaking, the exercise of social responsibility in the use of property, broad participation in political life, and a special concern for the poorest members of society—this is a promising basis around which to build bridges to many diverse people in the modern world. It is, further, an encouraging foundation upon which to form a consensus regarding what government policies, corporate practices, and private lifestyle choices might foster a better life for us all.

Perhaps this is the reason why all the popes since John XXIII have addressed their social encyclicals "to all people of good will," not merely to the world's Catholics. As a worldwide community of social concern, the Catholic Church is always eager to join in coalitions with like-minded people who seek to work together to promote peace, solidarity, and social justice. This path of cooperation is the most promising way that Catholic social teaching can be put into action.

As we have seen, it is helpful to think of Catholic social teaching as offering a yardstick we might use to measure the achievements or shortcomings of existing economic systems. This is a complex process, of course, and to do it thoroughly would involve amassing a huge amount of information about production, efficiency, distribution, and social conditions facing people who live under a given system. For example, before we can draw firm conclusions about whether a specific nation's economy is making an adequate "option for the poor," we would have to collect extensive data on employment opportunities, poverty patterns, demographic profiles, and social indicators such as infant mortality rates and life expectancy. Doing this type of "homework" is a daunting assignment, but it is not an impossible task. Indeed, it is a great service that we might hope will be performed by social scientists with increasing accuracy and ease in coming decades.

The task of using Catholic social teaching to measure the adequacy of economic systems is much easier in the abstract than in concrete settings. There is, of course, no space here to review the data on the actual achievements and outcomes of, say, capitalism in the United States during the 1920s or communism in the Soviet Union during the 1970s.

But it is possible briefly to review the basic commitments and value orientations of the general models of economic life contained in capitalism and communism. In the remainder of this chapter, we look at a simplified picture of each of these systems and draw a few preliminary judgments about the merits and defects of each system as viewed from the perspective of Catholic social teaching. Our conclusions will be modest and surely open to further debate, but might shed welcome light on the contribution of church positions to the great economic debates of our age.

One preliminary precaution is necessary. When we use broad terms such as "communism" and "capitalism," we are making sweeping generalizations about many actual practices that have unfolded over centuries. Each of these "-isms" has been practiced in numerous distinctive ways in a variety of contexts and places. To be truly accurate, we would have to precede each term with modifiers such as "early Maoist Communism," "New Deal liberal capitalism," or hybrids such as "1970s Swedish welfare-state democratic socialism." While the documents of Catholic social teaching occasionally contain statements that seem to address a few of these contexts, we would have to read between the lines in extremely creative ways before we could really claim that we were matching these documents to their intended audiences. Instead, let us simply admit that we are making broad-stroked applications of a few principles to the simplest models of communist and capitalist worldviews. Still, even this modest project can give us some useful insights about the strengths and inadequacies of these two rival systems.

The Catholic Critique of Communism

First, let us examine the core principles of communism. As it comes to us from the lineage of Karl Marx, Friedrich Engels, Vladimir Lenin, and Josef Stalin, Soviet-style Communism develops from a core commitment to end the alienation that traps most workers into oppression. The dominance of a class (the bourgeoisie) of rich owners of capital prevents the class of common laborers (the proletariat) from reaping a fair share of the benefits of their work. When people are thus robbed of the fruits of their labor, they become estranged from the work process, from themselves, and from the whole human race. What is required to reverse this process is an abrupt and complete revolution, in which the proletariat rises up to defeat the ruling bourgeoisie. Social structures are overturned to establish universal equality, not only of opportunities but also of outcomes. This new order is portrayed as a perfect world of harmony, where each person contributes according to his or her ability and receives according to his or her needs.

There are indeed a few praiseworthy aspects of communism evident in this brief and simple description. Using the principles of Catholic social teaching, we can applaud its high regard for the dignity of work and the call to protect the weakest members of society. The communist worldview portrays people as connected to one another with the bonds of solidarity. It takes seriously the necessity of recognizing the social responsibility that applies to property and the ways it is used. In communism, we find a serious commitment to empower the poor and to end the exploitation of the poor by the rich until greater equality is achieved. Thus, we can easily approve of its ultimate vision of a world where all can participate fully in social life and where material goods are shared so that all urgent human needs are satisfied.

But communism, as it was theorized by Marx and later spread by Soviet armies, contains many features that are objectionable from the standpoint of Catholic social teaching. First, there is no place for God in this system of thought. Marx's writings, in fact, have hostile things to say about the role of religion in increasing the oppression of the proletariat. Communist regimes that were established in the twentieth century were not only officially atheistic, but actively persecuted millions of Christians, Jews, and others whose attempts to practice their religion were declared counterrevolutionary. The tendency toward totalitarianism in communist regimes was fed by an insistence on the elimination of religious loyalties that were feared as a challenge to the complete and ultimate authority of the state.

A second set of objections concerns the way communism interprets the necessity of conflict in human history. Because it has a strong streak of determinism, communism asserts that we have no choice but to resolve the bitter relationship between the classes through a violent revolution in which the bourgeoisie is crushed. It despairs of reaching social agreement in which the rights of all are respected and in which compromises that benefit both workers and capitalists can be reached. There is no place for reconciliation between people divided by class boundaries, or for loving the sinner even as we strive to eliminate the sinful structures that cause oppression.

As a result of this harsh view of social relations, communist leaders demonstrated a willingness to use any means, including deception, torture, and mass murder of innocents, to advance the revolution. The atrocities that occurred at the time of the Russian Revolution and during later purges carried out under Stalin may be attributed to the vices of particular statesmen and military officers as well as to the inner logic of the communist system of thought. As the decades of oppression behind the Iron Curtain wore on, hardly anyone recalled Marx's original hope that eventually the state, once it had been cleansed of the poison of its former bourgeois masters, would wither away and leave all people with unprecedented freedom. The high ideals of the Revolution had been betrayed. Violent repression and stifling control over captive populations grew from a temporary means for attaining an idealistic vision to an end in itself and, eventually, to a brutal habit no communist regime could break.

A third set of objections concerns the strictly economic policies carried out by Soviet, Maoist, and most other versions of the communist creed. After any communist takeover, whether in Eastern Europe or Asia, industry was collectivized and all land and productive property became nationalized, usually without compensation to their former owners. Those entrusted with managing the new state monopolies were seldom sensitive to the true needs of the vast majority of the population. The well-being of the people as workers and consumers was largely ignored and their freedom of choice in products and careers was rarely a priority for the managers and bureaucrats who ran the corrupt systems. As antagonisms between people and their governments grew, dissenters were branded enemies of the state and persecuted mercilessly, with no regard for due process of the law.

Clearly, anyone whose reflections are guided by the lessons of Catholic social teaching cannot approve of these aspects of communism. Its disregard of human rights, its squelching of freedom of religion and conscience, and its promotion of violent solutions in the name of a materialistic revolution disqualify it as an acceptable approach to healthy life in society. However much we might be attracted to Marx's original vision of a utopia of universal worker solidarity in a world freed from alienation and exploitation, we have to admit that communism was among the greatest failures in all of human history. The seven decades of communist rule in the former Soviet Union alone cost many millions of lives and unleashed upon the world the horrors of a nuclear arms race during both the Cold War and several quite "hot" wars as well.

Still, we would be wise to pinpoint exactly which are the dangerous elements in the theories of Marx and his followers so that we may salvage any useful elements we might find there. As a matter of fact, Catholic social teaching is quite careful to distinguish between the objectionable and potentially useful insights of early socialists like Marx. In approaching this task, of course, much hinges upon how we view the relationship between socialism (as a general theory of social relations) and communism (just one concrete political movement that grew out of the early socialist theorists, many of whom were Christians).

This ambiguity is reflected in *Quadragesimo Anno*, the 1931 encyclical in which Pope Pius XI says, on the one hand, that socialism "is opposed to true Christianity" but, on the other hand, that "like all errors, socialism contains a certain element of truth" (no. 120). Four decades later, Paul VI would devote paragraph 33 of *Octogesima Adveniens* to a careful spelling out of four levels of Marxism as he understood it. While the Pope urges caution about the clearly unsuitable features of socialism, he also reminds us that it is a complex reality. He recognizes that some uses of socialist thought (especially as "a rigorous method of examining social and political reality") could be appropriate for Christians to adopt in their own social analysis. We should interpret these cautions from within the documents of Catholic social teaching as much needed reminders to look beyond mere labels to the real content of a political system, to seek to discover how people are actually treated by large social structures and the ideas behind them.

The Catholic Critique of Capitalism

When we turn to the task of using Catholic social teaching principles to evaluate capitalism, we have to consider a more nuanced picture. The dreams of capitalism are neither so noble nor its failures so obvious as those of its longtime communist rival. In its purest form, capitalism includes the principle of free enterprise (where there are no barriers to starting and running one's own business) and free-market exchange (private trading without government regulation or interference). Capitalism places a high value on the freedom of the individual to pursue his or her own self-interest. The favorite economic instrument of capitalist theory, of course, is the market, a mechanism that sets the price and quantity of goods and services in the most decentralized way possible. In a pure free market with perfectly free competition, millions of private decisions about the value of goods and services bid up or down their prices, so that no one person or group controls the buying and selling of goods.

To most of us, this brief sketch describes an extremely familiar reality, for we live in an age that takes markets for granted. But it would be an exaggeration to say that this is the only "natural" way for economic life to proceed. In many cultures and societies in human history, economic production, trade, and distribution were carefully regulated by central authorities. Even in medieval Europe, the dominant belief (supported by church officials and most theologians) was that justice required fixed prices and wages so that stability could be maintained. Only as the economy became modernized in recent centuries did fluctuating prices, as well as the practice of lending money at interest, become widely accepted. Our modern system of free-market capitalism grew out of a long evolution of the trading system through phases such as state-sponsored mercantilism, early colonialism, the Industrial Revolution, and finally the mass-consumption economy we have today.

Another face of capitalism worth mentioning here is "welfare-state capitalism." In the early 1900s, workers and their advocates won major victories in the U.S. and Europe in support of increased government regulation of the economy. Social movement such as the Progressive coalition in the U.S. campaigned successfully for such measures as shorter workdays and antitrust laws that curtailed monopolies and secretive price-fixing. These pioneering efforts to use government policy to pursue social justice were the birth of the modern welfare state whose protections we still enjoy. The U.S. eventually followed the lead of most European governments in expanding its role in protecting workers from the dire poverty that so often accompanied industrial accidents, illness, retirement, or unemployment. As popular support for income security and poor relief grew during the Great Depression, the Social Security Act of 1935 committed the federal government to providing survivors' benefits, pension plans, health insurance, and public assistance programs. Other protections for workers that are part of welfare-state efforts include minimum wage laws, safety and health regulations, legal recognition for labor union, and subsidies for family nutrition, job training, and educational entitlements.

Even though recent decades have witnessed the scaling back of these programs in most Western nations as costs mounted and public support for them evaporated, the phrase "welfare-state capitalism" is still an accurate description of most industrialized economies. But there are vocal critics of the remaining protections who want to see us move ever closer to a "free-market capitalism" with a much smaller role for government. Behind these proposals is an entire philosophy of economic life that is called *libertarianism*, or sometimes "neo-liberalism." Let us briefly examine the underlying principles behind this version of capitalism and evaluate a libertarian style of capitalism in the light of the principles of Catholic social teaching.

A libertarian worldview begins with the idea that personal freedom should be the highest value we seek in society. People are seen first of all as individuals responsible only to themselves. All larger groupings, such as families, cities, or nations, are merely artificial collections of individuals and, therefore, can make no claims upon people unless they consent voluntarily. The best form of government, it is argued, is the type that by and large gets out of the way and allows people to use their individual resources and property as desired. The free market is the natural mechanism to secure natural liberties, and any interference in these markets for capital or labor or products is unwelcome.

The contrast between this sketch of human social life and the worldview of Catholic social teaching is sharp. The libertarian perspective leaves no room for the virtue of solidarity, for the recognition that we really do belong to one another, and that our social groupings create more than just voluntary or accidental bonds. Catholic social teaching portrays government not as an unwelcome intruder upon our freedoms, but as the means by which we collectively and rightly act for social betterment. While libertarians seem confident that the "natural order" that arises spontaneously from the operation of free markets will be beneficial for all, any religiously grounded perspective would call attention to the imperative to build in some protections for the vulnerable. As markets produce winners and losers, what will happen to those who cannot compete successfully for jobs and goods?

These objections really boil down to a question of how we understand the basic qualities of the human person. Is each person to be understood as a consuming individual, as merely a bundle of selfish and infinite desires? Is our deepest identity wrapped up in becoming a fierce competitor in the game we call the modern economy? If so, we fall quickly into a destructive type of social Darwinism, where the principle of survival of the fittest divides the weak from the strong and relegates some people to the margins of existence, if not eliminating them altogether. The Catholic social principles of common good, participation, and solidarity are ignored when people, no matter how well intentioned, adopt social standards that place the value of liberty too high above the value of basic equality.

Libertarians often defend their free-market positions as necessary conditions for creating the maximum amount of wealth, maintaining economic incentives for people to work hard, and promoting the value of efficiency, so that all resources are used in the most productive ways. Because it so emphasizes the efficiency that it claims can come only from free markets, this pure form of capitalism sharply opposes any type of planning that might reserve some resources for the poor, such as income entitlements or health care guarantees. The fear of a centralized system that controls our economic life is so strong among libertarians that commonsense measures to provide for the common good, such as publicly coordinated industrial policies and infrastructure improvements, are spurned as dangerous. All too often, libertarians ignore the objection that if these necessary social functions are not done in a democratic way through government legislation, then solutions may be done only by default by a small elite of the most powerful.

Even many of those who praise the market would admit that if markets are left unchecked by government regulation, numerous desirable activities would remain altogether undone. The list of such "market failures" and "public goods" includes pollution control, the maintenance of parks and roads, the checking of monopolies, regional planning, the alleviation of poverty, and other tasks that contribute to good public order. In a strictly libertarian world, practically nothing would ever happen that is not motivated by the thirst for profits. Guided by Catholic social teaching, we can easily identify numerous social necessities that require a more well-rounded approach to social life.

It turns out, not surprisingly, that a majority of those who call themselves libertarians are the very people who benefit most from free markets. They are, for the most part, the "winners" in the competition that is made more fierce by means of increased reliance on unregulated markets. Imagine, for example, a Wall Street trader whose chief skill is to manipulate the financial markets every day in pursuit of the winning formula for investing capital in the most profitable corporations and business ventures. Of course, many play this high-stakes game and lose disastrously, but imagine for a moment one of the "stock market whizzes" who consistently makes fortunes (for himself and perhaps for some rich backers as well). He vehemently defends the huge personal rewards he reaps as fair payment for the skills he has developed and the service he provides to investors and entrepreneurs. Whenever he hears suggestions that financial markets should be more closely regulated, he opposes such ideas as dangerous interference with the natural order of the universe.

Occasionally our imaginary trader will find himself encountering, as we all do from time to time, others whose life experiences lead them to different conclusions about what is desirable in economics. A chance encounter with someone of another social class might challenge his libertarian worldview. Maybe it will be a street person, one of the many thousands whom the unregulated housing market has priced out of his last home and into a horribly uncertain future. Maybe it will be the low-paid janitor at his office building or a financially strapped cousin he meets at a family reunion. It could be in any setting and on any occasion when casual conversations reveal how the unfair structure of educational and work opportunities exclude so many from the comfortable mainstream of society.

You might want to allow your imagination to fill in the details of these conversations between such people who have received very different treatments at the hands of markets. What topics might come up regarding the fairness of economic structures, realistic life chances, and huge gaps in social status? Would one of the privileged "winners" be able to defend in a credible way the reasons why the system has favored his skills over the labors of the hardworking blue-collar employee? How might the topics of efficiency, incentive, and fair returns for effort be debated in this conversation?

Of course, there is nothing conclusive about this example, but it may be a helpful "thought experiment" to reveal the real-life implications of the most radical defenses of free-market capitalism. While the ideas of "cowboy capitalism" and unhindered competition seem to have growing appeal in our society today, the luster of the ideal of free markets is tarnished as soon as we consider the plight of the losers. How will we make adequate provisions for those whose contribution is not highly valued in labor markets? What concerns for human values and social justice should check our enthusiasm for uninhibited financial freedom?

These drawbacks of the extreme form of libertarianism should by no means lead us to reject all forms of capitalism. The more moderate versions (such as welfare-state capitalism) that include some regulation of markets to insure that they serve human priorities are quite constructive and generally deserving of much support. That this support is always conditional, depending upon many local factors, is a point reiterated by Pope John Paul II in his 1991 encyclical *Centesimus Annus:*

> The church has no models to present; models that are real and truly effective can only arise within the framework of different historical situations through the efforts of all those who responsibly confront concrete problems in all their social, economic, political and cultural aspects . . . For such a task, the church offers her social teaching as an indispensable and ideal orientation, a teaching which, as already mentioned, recognizes the positive value of the market and of enterprise, but which at the same time points out that these need to be oriented toward the common good (no. 43).

With John Paul II, our assessment of capitalism is a mixed bag. We of course approve of its high regard for human liberty and resistance to any form of totalitarianism, but must remain concerned about how easily it slides into indifference to the needs of others. As has often been said, the market is a fine servant but a bad master. In so far as it sparks human creativity and allows us to contribute to the good life in society without undue interference, it measures up quite well to most of the principles of Catholic social teaching. But when extreme versions of free-market capitalist ideology are used to justify crass materialism, selfishness, and indifference to the plight of the weaker members of society, it is then that we find ourselves objecting to some of its features.

Applying Catholic Social Teaching in the Real World

This chapter has allowed us to look at the complexities of a few of the many "-isms" that dominate the way political scientists and economists view life in society. We have used Catholic social teaching as an alternative worldview that helps us identify some of the positive and negative features of communism and capitalism in their pure forms. But, as we all know, the real world of actual economic life is even more complicated than these pure abstract models might suggest. Each nation and region has a mix of various "-isms" as well as many distinctive institutions that it has inherited from previous generations. Even those of us who agree on the principles of Catholic social teaching must constantly update our judgments about how well any given economic or political system measures up to the standards and values it recommends.

An additional challenge is to recognize the simple fact that dominant systems are slow to change. Because we cannot expect the basic structure of the economy in a given country to be altered overnight, Catholic social teaching is perhaps most often helpful when we use it as a guide for advocating gradual changes in the existing system. It is a tool that allows us to expose and correct injustices, whether dramatic or ordinary in their occurrence. People of faith can use the Church's social teaching as a starting point for dialogue about how to make the economy more humane so that it better reflects the values and principles of peace, justice, and compassion. It gives us the broad outlines of a picture of a proper order for the world. From this picture we can challenge governments, corporations, and individuals to reflect these values in their laws, practices, and choices. There will inevitably be disagreements about which precise goals to adopt and which strategies to utilize, but a solid commitment to this quest is something all are called to live out.

Perhaps, in the end, this chapter leaves us with more questions than answers. If there is no blueprint to follow in the search for justice, what are we to do? Applying Catholic social teaching to the real world can touch our lives in many ways beyond reflecting on the big "-isms" that usually play out on levels far above our heads. More basically, it is a matter of pursing a lifestyle of peace and justice, and of exercising social responsibility on the most local of levels. Here we naturally think of heroic actions for justice, often performed by people we greatly admire: prophets, popes, missionaries, and politicians who speak out for justice. We certainly need these high-profile people to make their important impact on the world. But the cause of social justice also needs ordinary people, like each of us, to influence our small corners of the world in positive ways.

Mother Teresa, a hero to millions, was famous for calling her admirers to "find your own Calcutta." By this she meant that it is important, wherever you find yourself, to take advantage of whatever opportunities arise for social involvement and work for justice. Even when the ways of justice we choose seem quite ordinary, extremely local, and far from heroic, they may be precisely what God is calling us to do at this moment.

Take, for example, the story of St. Peter Claver (1581–1654). He started out as an ordinary Spanish Jesuit of his day but, almost by accident, found himself ministering to some of the most oppressed people on earth—thousands of

Africans kidnapped and being sold into servitude in the slave markets of Cartagena, Colombia. Peter Claver dreamed about single-handedly ending the institution of slavery and dramatically confronting the entire seventeenth-century establishment of colonialism that supported the many cruelties he witnessed. But he was limited to what he could realistically do: make simple visits to the slave ships and prisons where he could console, counsel, and offer the sacraments to those deprived of their freedom and dignity. Over his forty years of ministry, St. Peter Claver baptized some 300,000 slaves. By showing these men, women, and children the respect owed to children of God, he certainly did contribute to the change in attitude that eventually abolished the slave trade. The evil "-isms" of his day were not vulnerable to direct attack by a single person, but eventually were conquered by the power of love and compassion that issued forth in acts of justice.

In the end, living out the message of Catholic social teaching is largely about reexamining and purifying our loyalties. It challenges us to ask hard questions about the things we love and are willing to make sacrifices for. Are these things merely self-serving or do they include a wider circle of concern? Do our earthly goals somehow relate to our religious beliefs or is God excluded from the majority of our everyday concerns?

We have seen that the dangers of communism and capitalism include a warping of proper values so that goals such as the pursuit of profits, efficient markets, class-based revolution, or the national interest come to take the place of the things that truly deserve our deepest loyalties. Catholic social teaching contains important reminders that no humanly constructed system will ever completely capture the only objects worthy of our full loyalty: the God we love and the people God creates and redeems. This is the wellspring and motivation for all our efforts to create the conditions that will allow people throughout the world to flourish as God intends, through an order of peace and justice that benefits all humankind.

Questions for Reflection

1. Imagine you are in a room with three people and each of them is making a different argument about Catholic social teaching. The first supports communist collectivism, since (he argues) socialist measures are the logical outcome of all this talk about the common good. The second claims that Catholic social teaching is really a blanket vindication of free-market capitalism. The third claims that Catholic social teaching is a distinctive "third way" between capitalism and communism. How would

you respond to these three voices? Which is closest to the truth, or are all three equally misguided?

2. In your experience of work and the marketplace, do you find our capitalist system mostly a constructive way of organizing life or mostly in need of change? Do its defects outweigh its advantages? If so, would you recommend gradual reforms or is a drastic about-face required to make the capitalist economy better serve human needs?

3. Use your imagination to construct a dialogue between the imaginary libertarian-minded Wall Street trader (see page 194) and one of his less fortunate neighbors. What topics might come up? Is either one likely to experience a change of mind or heart?

4. How do you interpret the events of 1989–1990, when the Berlin Wall fell and the Soviet communist bloc crumbled? Did this revolution indicate the utter failure of all forms of socialism or just one particular type of communist-style socialism? Can we in the capitalist West still learn any valuable lessons from socialist theory?

5. Can you think of any individuals or movements that advocate for economic change in today's capitalist order? Do you admire their work or do you have reservations about their approach?

Chapter 7

The Future of Catholic Social Teaching

This final chapter attempts to look ahead to possible future developments in Catholic social teaching. Of course, it is always dangerous to offer predictions about the future, since unforeseeable occurrences have a way of upsetting our neat expectations. In attempting to chart the future course of Catholic social teaching, it seems safe to say that we can expect a mix of change and continuity. This chapter makes an effort to identify the most likely developments in the years ahead.

Four Continuities:
Further Shifts in Emphasis

Like many traditions of thought, Catholic social teaching has updated itself by undergoing a certain amount of change in both its message and the style in which the message is presented. This does not mean that the Church has denied or overturned what it previously taught; rather, it has refined its message to better meet the needs of changing times and to dialogue with new currents of thought. In this section, we examine four examples of how Catholic social teaching has updated itself in recent years. None of the four involves a tale about some completely new principle or idea displacing older teachings. Rather, each is about a shift of emphasis or a new way of talking about familiar concerns as the Church addresses a rapidly changing world. In each of these four areas, we can expect even further refinements in the coming years, as the tradition of Catholic social teaching continues to grow and mature.

1. Personalism

The first of these shifts has been toward an approach called *personalism*. It is difficult to define this word, because the term has been applied to various schools of philosophical thought in different times and places. Interestingly, one of the hotbeds of personalism was the University of Lublin in Poland, in the very department where Karol Wojtyla, the future Pope John Paul II, taught in the 1950s. At the heart of personalism is a deep concern for the value of the human person, especially as it is threatened by the large structures (such as government and powerful corporations) through which modern life is organized. To be a personalist is to measure all things—including changes in culture, technology, and systems of production—by their contribution to the well-being of persons. The messages of many personalists include an appeal to reawaken interest in spirituality and the religious dimension of human life, challenging us to look beyond the level of strictly material needs and their fulfillment.

Notice how closely this description of personalism overlaps with several themes of Catholic social teaching, especially its emphasis on human dignity and rights. In this sense, a personalist flavor has always been present in modern church teachings on life in society. However, it is only in recent years, especially since Pope John Paul II started mentioning personalism by name in his social encyclicals, that it has received greater attention in church circles.

As is true with the remaining three themes, the increasing prominence of personalism in Catholic social teaching represents not something drastically new but, rather, the further development of a helpful strand that was already present in the inner logic of the Church's social message. Because the term personalism captures so many of the concerns the Church seeks to underline in its teachings about human society, we may certainly expect an even more obvious and deliberate use of personalist thought in future social encyclicals.

Personalism is at its most helpful when it guides our attempts to balance the extremes of a radical individualism (the blind spot to which capitalist systems are prone) and collectivism (one of the errors of communism). If we go too far in either of these directions, our approach to life is incomplete and potentially harmful to ourselves and others. This is precisely the message that John Paul II applies to the field of human work in the 1981 encyclical *Laborem Exercens*. In paragraph 15 (a section of the text that bears the label "The Personalist Argument"), the Pope explains his defense of the "priority of labor over capital" by focusing on the way people are treated in such places as factories and large corporations. On the one hand, the dignity of each person should not be dwarfed by such huge structures that threaten to gobble up our individuality. On the other hand, we should not emphasize our individual rights so strongly that we lose all sense of social responsibility and our willingness to make sacrifices for the good of larger groups. Because personalist thought helps us maintain this important balance, we should warmly welcome further explicit use of personalism in future Catholic social teaching documents.

2. Humility before the Data of Social Analysis

This theme concerns the attitude or method of recent church social teachings. The growing trend worth noticing here is perhaps best summarized by the phrase "humility before the data." While an older style of proceeding might have favored making firm church pronouncements on social issues, with a strong sense of certainty about its positions, the more recent style emphasizes caution and modesty about the judgments we make.

As we have consistently seen above, the Church is hesitant to lay down firm stances on complex social issues, preferring instead to see its task here as one of informing the consciences of people as they form their own opinions. This observation becomes especially obvious when we contrast social teaching with the Church's more clear-cut stipulations in the field of sexual ethics. All the documents of Catholic social teaching since the 1960s have recognized the possibility of legitimate differences of opinion and the need for ongoing social analysis, that is, the method of gaining knowledge about political and economic life that we explored in chapter four.

Another way of explaining this second theme is to say that Catholic social teaching has grown toward a greater appreciation of the limits of natural law. (Recall from chapter four that natural law is a way of making ethical judgments that is based on the expectation that God's will is somehow discoverable in the structures of nature). In the past, the Church exhibited more confidence that the conclusions it drew from using natural law reasoning were fixed and final. Recent decades, however, have witnessed such rapid social change that the need for ongoing social analysis and data collection could no longer be ignored.

A good example of this shift concerns the Church's stance on the legitimacy of private property. As we saw in chapter five, the earliest social encyclicals cited natural law to affirm the general principle that private ownership of property is God's firm intention for the created world. Yet later documents came to recognize a number of legitimate exceptions to recognizing unlimited property rights. What accounts for this change is a growing awareness of the complexity of social relations in various regional contexts around the world. This shift is reflected in a change of style in the more recent documents of Catholic social teaching. Whereas the oldest documents used a deductive style (a "top-down" way of reasoning from universal principles to local applications), the newer ones are more inductive (using "bottom-up" reasoning that is more likely to respect local variations and special needs). We can expect this trend to continue for the simple reason that the world of human society is not likely to halt its dizzying rate of change.

3. Awareness of Social Sin

A third development that we can expect to continue is the recent emphasis on social sin. Since the 1970s, several of the documents of Catholic social teaching have expressed concern about "structures of evil" that surround all people and in which we all too often take part. A key example of such an evil social structure is racial discrimination—blatant unfairness toward minority groups and their members. Although we are free as individuals to refuse this temptation, the accumulated weight of racial bias exerts an indisputable influence on our cultural environment. The sheer act of living in a society that perpetuates such destructive patterns of thought and action makes it quite likely that each one of us will somehow fall prey to the sin of racism, even if in subtle ways. Other evil structures treated in recent encyclicals include imperialism and colonialism—patterns of activity that have harmed millions of people and in which millions of others have cooperated over many centuries.

The point of talking about social sin is not to make us feel guilty about injustices we are hardly responsible for and situations we merely inherited from previous generations. In fact, to truly qualify as a "sin" in the usual sense of the word, an act of racial bias or some other form of injustice must be deliberately chosen by an individual who acts with impure motives and at least some awareness of the harm being inflicted. Pope John Paul II is careful to remind us that the root of social sin is always in personal sin and the evil choices of individuals, which come before the spread of evil to large social institutions and practices. Nevertheless, since Catholic social teaching began speaking about social sin, it has made a real contribution to our reflections about the barriers to achieving true justice in the world today. Calling attention to the evils that are already present in social structures may help to motivate us to make the desperately needed changes that will benefit those harmed by destructive patterns of behavior. It may succeed in challenging us to move beyond the temptation of apathy to a sincere commitment to urgent social change.

By spreading the message about social sin, the Church invites us to engage in some form of "consciousness-raising," that is, a change in attitude and a desire to learn more about the world's problems. The result hopefully will be that all listeners will increase their awareness of evil social structures and will be motivated to take action to end these unfair situations. Few of us are called to be famous prophets who denounce injustice in public arenas, but our Christian vocations always include a call to practice the virtue of courage and to challenge the *status quo* in some way.

Sadly, the Church's call to resist social sin has so far largely failed to capture the imagination of most of the faithful. Rare indeed is the priest who ever hears a penitent express remorse over participating in evil structures, such as clubs or organizations that practice racism, sexism, or elitism. All too seldom do we reflect on the indirect but important effects of our economic actions, such as purchasing garments sewn by child laborers or investing in companies that dump toxic wastes. It is doubtful whether any advertising executive has ever stepped into a confessional to discuss his or her abuses of the public trust in promoting misleading commercials for an overly profit-hungry corporation. As the quip goes, when we think about sin, most of us imagine the bedroom, not the boardroom! In other words, most of our awareness of sin and practice of sacramental confession remains squarely focused on the level of strictly individual or at most interpersonal acts, but rarely on the level of our larger-scale involvements in social institutions such as corporations.

Nor is this situation likely to change anytime soon. It will be a constant challenge to future popes, bishops, clergy, and lay people to find ways to talk to their neighbors about the need for sharper awareness of social responsibility. In the present climate of apathy, it is a tall order to encourage greater participation in movements to change the *status quo* by seeing the world with a keen eye for exposing injustices in large-scale structures.

Of course, the easiest path for most people is to keep their faith private and to ignore the urgent need for Christians, as a necessary requirement of their faith in Jesus Christ, to increase their involvement in public affairs. We can hope that church officials will continue to use Catholic social teaching as a vehicle for expressing the call to both individual and social holiness. To ignore either dimension is to cut our faith in half. Future social encyclicals may continue to be a privileged place where church teaching might bridge the local and the global, and express the need to examine ever more closely unjust aspects of the structures and institutions we so often take for granted.

4. Public Theology and Concerns about Credible Witness

The fourth and final item on our list of shifts in Catholic social teaching is the new emphasis on the public role of Christian theology in the broader society. Obviously, this development is closely related to the attention to structural evil we just discussed, for it involves the task of engaging the whole society along with its largest structures, and not just Christians as isolated individuals, in order to pursue justice in the fullest way possible. This shift toward a more complete public face of the Church is neither a brand new development nor an achievement we are close to completing. Rather, it is an ongoing task in which the Church's efforts have been unfolding since the beginning of Christianity. Recall that we explored many issues relevant to this task of "doing public theology" in chapter two. There we examined several questions and positions that naturally arise when any age tries to answer the famous metaphorical question of Tertullian: "What does Jerusalem have to say to Athens?"

But let us focus on a few issues that have arisen in recent years concerning the way Catholic social teaching has been able to engage public life in our contemporary cultural setting. One significant development has been a noticeable antagonism between some Christian voices and certain aspects of popular culture. In standing up boldly for important principles such as the dignity of all human life, spokespersons for Catholicism as well as Protestant Christianity have found themselves in a stance of denouncing certain currents of thought that have become common in the cultural mainstream.

The most ringing phrase that echoes in these recent public conversations is the accusation that we are witnessing a "culture of death." This calls attention to the many ways, including public policies and private practices such as abortion, euthanasia, and capital punishment, that society has exhibited an attitude of callousness toward human life. The principle of the dignity of human life, so prominent in the documents of Catholic social teaching, seems to be under massive attack when decisions are made with increasing frequency to terminate lives that are considered a threat, an inconvenience, or a burden to others. Perhaps the boldest denunciation of these horrifying trends appears in Pope John Paul II's 1995 encyclical letter *Evangelium Vitae* ("The Gospel of Life"). Here the Pope reviews and extends such arguments as those we encountered from Chicago's late Cardinal Joseph Bernardin, who called for a "consistent ethic of life." Pope John Paul's efforts are part of a passionate struggle to speak a prophetic word against the distorted values that promote death rather than life. The calling of all Christians, he asserts, is to resist the "culture of death" by creating a "culture of life" grounded in the gospel.

By challenging the "culture of death," our church leaders seem to be making a choice to play the prophet, not in the sense of predicting the future but in the sense of challenging injustice even at the price of their own popularity. But it would be a serious mistake to interpret this choice of the "prophetic option" as somehow eliminating the "dialogue option" that has for the most part characterized the recent relationship between Catholic theology and modern culture. Even as it spends time and energy criticizing destructive aspects of secular culture, Catholic social teaching renews its commitment to engage, teach, and learn from what is helpful in that culture. In fact, although they barely make an appearance in most official church documents, a number of pressing concerns about how to strengthen the "dialogue option" has received much attention in church circles in recent years.

Perhaps the best way to summarize these concerns is to say that many in the Church today are worried about the credibility of the Church's public witness. If hardly anyone is willing to take seriously what the Church says about peace and justice, then it becomes doubtful whether Catholic social teaching can really fulfill its mission. The solution cannot be, of course, to change the content of the Church's message just to win a more favorable audience. This type of compromise would be like surrendering the core of the gospel message to fit the latest fashion—a serious betrayal of the mission of the Church. In other words, it is an important sign of vitality and fidelity to its mission that the Church keeps open the "prophetic option," even when this strains some relationships with those who are accomplices to the "culture of death."

So, as we look to the future, what steps can the Church take to increase its public credibility without altering its prophetic messages about social justice? The most important items involve measures that would, so to speak, take ammunition away from those who claim that the Catholic Church is guilty of blatant hypocrisy. These vocal critics find fault with the Church for not practicing in its internal policies and procedures all the elements of the justice message it preaches. Until the Church "gets its own house in order," they warn, it will not have earned sufficient credibility to be an effective public witness to the gospel. In fact, from time to time church voices have publicly echoed this very concern. For example, *Justitia in Mundo*, the social teaching document from the 1971 Synod of Bishops, declared that "anyone who ventures to speak to people about justice must first be just in their eyes" (no. 40).

The closing pages of this book do not contain adequate space to treat all the objections that arise, nor does this author pretend to possess the wisdom to offer definitive solutions to the problems highlighted by these critics of the Church. But it might be helpful to offer at least a partial list of the complaints that are allegedly creating this credibility gap. Of course, all these items are a matter of perception; different people might look at the same facts and make very different judgments about their significance. While some observers would claim that rapid change is urgently needed in several areas of church life, others would conclude that "if it's not broke, don't attempt to fix it." But in any case, let us look at three of the issues that cannot be ignored as the Church attempts to win a fair and sympathetic hearing for its social teaching and continue its important task of dialogue with the modern world.

At the top of any such a list of credibility issues facing the Church today is the question of gender equality and the treatment of women within the Catholic Church. Charges about sexism in church practices are especially prevalent in the Western nations with the most advanced feminist movements, and go far beyond the controversy over whether women are eligible to be ordained as priests or deacons. Both male and female critics of church practices accuse officials of excluding women from meaningful participation in ecclesiastical decisions and blocking their rightful access to positions of authority. Even the very documents of Catholic social teaching are sometimes read as part of the problem, as they seem to some critics to belittle the contributions of women and enshrine an old-fashioned family ideal that prevents women from advancing. Even without entering into the complex debate about the merit of these accusations, we can certainly say that the Church should work hard in the years ahead to change these perceptions and the realities behind them. Until women are able to recognize in Catholic teaching the real world of their daily struggles, the Church's social message will fall on many deaf and disbelieving ears.

A second cause for concern about the credibility of the Church relates to labor issues, an area where Catholic social teaching has been a beacon of light in professing the rights of workers. The problem is that, directly or indirectly, the Church employs millions of workers who do not always receive the best possible treatment. In recent years, specifically, controversy has swirled around the adequacy of the pay scales and fringe benefits received by those who work in schools, hospitals, and other institutions sponsored by the Catholic Church and its religious orders of priests, brothers, and nuns. In some cases, church officials have encountered unfavorable publicity when union organizers pointed out to them the discrepancy between Catholic documents supporting the right to form labor unions and the actual practice of some church-based institutions that discourage unionization.

Until the values of worker rights and full participation (which are clearly proclaimed in the documents of Catholic social teaching) are fully reflected in actual labor practices within the Church, this stumbling block of perceived hypocrisy will remain.

A third challenge to Catholic social teaching involves the internal life of the Church, including the very procedures by which the teaching documents are written. Some critics claim that the Church needs to take a hard look at the way it conducts its study of social issues and shapes its response to the problems of today's world. They argue that achieving broader consultation in drafting the documents that become Catholic social teaching would enhance the credibility of the public witness of the Church. In order to understand these suggestions, let us take a look at some of the underlying concerns about the actual writing of the documents of Catholic social teaching.

You may have noticed that the previous chapters are careful to refer to the teaching efforts of popes in terms of "publishing encyclicals" rather than "writing encyclicals." These words must be chosen carefully because the issue of actual authorship of the documents of Catholic social teaching raises some problems. In most cases, we possess limited knowledge of precisely who it was that actually penned the final words. Upon first glance, it may seem dishonest for a pope to claim credit for writing a document that contains words that are not his own. But recall that encyclicals appear in the form of letters addressed to members of the Church and are offered as pastoral and practical assistance in their lives. It only makes sense for popes facing this daunting task to consult with the appropriate experts, so that the best possible letter may be composed and published over the signature of the pope himself.

Recall that Table 1, page 78, includes a list of twelve documents. I explained in chapter 3 that two of these documents are from groups of bishops *(Gaudium et Spes* and *Justitia in Mundo)* In the case of several of the other ten encyclicals, certain clues have surfaced about how the document was actually written. Most often, popes seem to have relied on an inner circle of a few advisors who contributed to successive drafts of encyclicals, often over many months of work. We should not be surprised to hear that most of these aides have been members of religious orders or priests with specialized knowledge of economics, political theory, and the social sciences. In some cases, popes have given wide latitude to their chosen experts, asking only to see semi-completed drafts as they neared completion. Other popes, particularly those with more scholarly backgrounds, have preferred a hands-on management style and have undertaken a great deal of the actual writing themselves. In general, the research and writing of social encyclicals have progressed under the veil of strict confidentiality, with a prevailing policy of silence about the drafting process. Most contributors have been remarkably discreet about their assistance even decades after their involvement.

Being aware of these procedures raises questions about the possible benefits of wider participation in the process by which social teaching is developed. Some ask whether it is desirable for a document that will represent the entire world-wide church to be written in relative secrecy by just a handful of people who work at the Vatican. Various arguments for and against the current approach might appeal to different people.

In the search for alternative models, we might turn to the history of four documents already mentioned. Two documents in Table 1 (*Gaudium et Spes* from Vatican II and *Justitia in Mundo* from the 1971 Synod of Bishops) were written by large committees composed primarily of bishops and their advisors during the course of worldwide gatherings of church leaders. We have also referred to two pastoral letters from the Bishops' Conference of the United States: "Economic Justice for All" and "The Challenge of Peace." Each went through a lengthy process in which several early drafts were released in order to invite public feedback. In a remarkable spirit of open dialogue, the committee of bishops in charge of each letter sponsored listening sessions in which many dozens of experts were invited to comment on the subject. Many people expressed great enthusiasm for such an open process that consulted broadly and publicly over such a considerable length of time.

Clearly, a happy balance needs to be struck between the extreme models presented by papal encyclicals on the one hand and the American bishops' recent pastoral letters on the other. One issue is timeliness; it took the U.S. bishops six long years to complete the two letters, after an initial commitment to the task in 1980. While many people were genuinely excited about their roles in helping to improve each draft of the letters on peace and economic justice, it must be admitted that there is a diminishing usefulness to any project that lasts too long. It may seem like trying to hit a moving target; by the time you agree to a shared description of the problem, the problem itself may have significantly changed. Vatican II surely did us a tremendous service by adding to the traditional model of the "teaching" Church a new model of the "learning" Church. However, we still struggle with the challenge of finding the most effective ways for the Church to accomplish its task of listening and learning from events and voices in the wider society.

We should also be aware of the constant dangers of attempting to write any document by means of a committee. The best insights and contributions tend to become watered down in a process of compromise that seeks to please all partners. This can become a major drawback when attempting to produce documents that exhibit a unity of vision and clarity of purpose, as do the best encyclicals. The desire for broader consultation on social teaching is clearly a genuine and constructive guide to future efforts. But it still remains unclear precisely how best to achieve wider participation in shaping the stance our Church will take on social issues in the new millennium.

We have now completed our list of four significant shifts in recent Catholic social teaching, as well as our examination of three challenges the Church must face in order to be as credible as possible as it participates in public dialogue today. To this list of the three challenges we might add other areas where the Church might grow toward greater internal justice: eliminating abuses such as clericalism, excessively centralized hierarchy, and the exclusion of minority voices that are too seldom heard by high church officials. Until all these problems are addressed, we should avoid any uncritical celebration of the Church's contribution to public life and the ongoing debates regarding social issues. Only by making progress in all these areas will the Church in the years ahead find itself a truly effective advocate of the values it professes: freedom, democracy, human rights, the broad sharing of opportunities, and the equal dignity of all God's children.

Two New Challenges: The Environment and Postindustrialism

This chapter began with a promise to make some significant predictions about the future of Catholic social teaching. So far we have hardly "gone out on a limb" in venturing forecasts, since the four trends treated above are merely continuations of already established trends in church teaching. That easy part of the job must now be followed by the harder task of predicting some themes that will, without benefit of much advance fanfare, become important in future documents of Catholic social teaching. Here I will gamble on just two developments that might begin to loom large in the years ahead.

The first is the area of *environmental concern*. Although care for the earth is a theme that fits easily with the call to social responsibility within Catholic social teaching, it is surprising how seldom ecological concerns are actually mentioned in the encyclicals. There are practically no sections of the social teaching documents that offer an extended treatment of what it means to practice "environmental justice." So to predict that future Catholic social teaching will begin to tackle the topic of ecology does indeed involve an element of risk, since there are few previous signs of interest in this topic on the part of Vatican officials.

Yet my guess about this future direction for Catholic social teaching is a gamble that is likely to pay off, for a number of reasons. First, there is a growing worldwide consensus that damage to the environment is reaching a critical point as we begin the twenty-first century. Although there have been significant efforts and movements for ecological improvement for many decades, our misuse of the resources of the earth has left our waters and atmosphere crying out for renewed attention. It is a set of urgent challenges which can no longer be ignored by individuals or the groups they belong to, including churches and faith-based nonprofit organizations.

Second, there are already some initial hints that the message of environmental concern is beginning to take root in the minds of some church leaders, especially on the local level. Many parishes and dioceses have adopted programs to raise awareness of pollution and to organize efforts to preserve our fragile ecosystem. Local campaigns to expand recycling, encourage organic farming, and raise funds to preserve the world's shrinking rain forests have often been started or cosponsored by churches. These programs and efforts have made an important impact on the lives of many people of faith, feeding their spirituality and rekindling their commitment to a life of discipleship. Many parishioners express hope that their grassroots efforts will capture the attention of high church officials and make their way into the teachings of popes and bishops.

But there is a third reason we might express confidence about a future flowering of environmental concern within the Church: it simply makes a lot of sense to expect this to happen. When we consider all the rich themes of Catholic social teaching, it is a natural outgrowth of its messages about justice to extend our practice of social responsibility to concerns about the environment. That is why the relative silence of the Church on these matters up until now is so surprising The earth is a gift from God we share with all other creatures, so it is obvious that our relationship to other beings, human or not, is affected by the physical environment. To show disregard for the air that others breathe and the quality of the water they drink is to damage not only inanimate objects but also our relationships with living things. Wasting and polluting precious natural resources is sinful for it is an offense against the things and people God has blessed us with. To be concerned about the effect of all my actions on the fragile ecosystem is to nurture an attitude of care for others that is most consistent with the core messages of Catholic social teaching.

It is interesting to speculate on the possible shape of future church statements about the environment. Some clues may be found in recent documents on the environment published by national and regional groups of bishops, including statements from the Philippines, Australia, Italy, the United States, and various parts of Latin America. These letters, along with a few writings and addresses from the Vatican on this topic, seem to be struggling to make a transition from a troubling older theory of the environment to a newer and more promising approach. Let us see what is at stake in these contrasting perspectives on ecology.

The older approach is sometimes called the "stewardship model." It portrays humans as the rightful masters of creation, placed in the center of the world, and presented by God with the gift of nearly absolute dominion over the universe. In the few places where documents of Catholic social teaching mention the natural environment, they interpret the Book of Genesis in a way that encourages people to subdue the earth and claim its resources for the sole purpose of human improvement. For example, *Gaudium et Spes* contains the thought:

> For man [and woman], created to God's image, received a mandate to subject to [themselves] the earth and all that it contains, and to govern the world with justice and holiness (no. 34).

Following this view does not necessarily make us oblivious to ecological damage, but it does tend to restrict our concern to only human well-being. As evidence that the spotlight is clearly on humans (although the noninclusive language of the original text of the document suggests a focus on only the male half of the human race!), note this sentence from *Octogesima Adveniens:*

> [People are] suddenly becoming aware that by an ill-considered exploitation of nature [they] risk destroying it and becoming in [their] turn the victim of this degradation (no. 21).

The focus of concern is clearly on humans; the outcome of any other victims, such as species of animals or entire ecosystems, remains at best an afterthought.

A more adequate and updated approach would take more seriously the intrinsic value of nonhuman created things. It would get beyond the inordinate bias, sometimes called *species-ism* or *anthropocentrism*, that may belittle the worth and beauty of nature. A more thorough reverence for creation would allow us to imagine a type of solidarity that extends beyond the limits of the human species to include other forms of life and the places they inhabit as well. The divine plan for the universe is frustrated not just when our acts boomerang and cause harm to humans, but whenever they destroy the environment in irreparable ways. The challenge is to begin to measure our acts, such as damming rivers, felling forests, and developing land for commercial use, in a more holistic manner in terms of their ecological impact.

It is one thing to predict that Catholic social teaching will someday grow beyond the stewardship model to a more ecologically sensitive approach, but it is a much more difficult task to imagine what guidance it will give for balancing "care for persons" and "care for the environment." After all, every step of any form of progress involves some costs, and every economic advance gobbles up some natural resources. How to weigh the benefits of future economic growth against the costs of pollution and resource depletion is a difficult question and can become a divisive issue, pitting human needs against the well-being of the natural world as varying priorities are debated. It would be a great contribution to both Church and world if future documents of Catholic social teaching would offer some insightful guidelines for making these important decisions. The Church's tradition of speaking so forcefully about the sacredness of life, universal solidarity, and the common good gives it a head start in forming constructive and credible teachings in the area of environmental concern.

The second of our two future challenges can be treated more briefly. It involves the evolving shape of the economy and the ways that new systems of production will treat millions of people. As anyone who reads the newspaper surely knows, new patterns of world trade, computer technology, and machine automation have greatly altered the way goods are produced and valued. The computer age has even created a whole new category of "information goods," such as computer software and data bases. It has also launched a new class of "knowledge workers," those who make their living as systems analysts, programmers, and consultants. We are moving rapidly into the dizzying world of what is often called the "postindustrial society." This awkward phrase is not to imply that we will soon have no industries at all but, rather, that the dominant trend is toward an automated style of production that is rapidly turning the assembly-line worker into an economic dinosaur.

The problem with all these advances is that they threaten to leave millions, even billions, of people behind. While we in the First World celebrate the growing conveniences of a "consumer lifestyle" now served by the internet and the Web, the vast majority of the world's people, especially those in the poorest lands, can only dream of access to these wonders. Even more disturbing is the growing evidence that this new economic order is systematically wiping out the types of manufacturing and blue-collar jobs that less educated workers in every land generally rely upon for their livelihood.

In some cases, automation and information technologies are eliminating entire categories of jobs. In other instances, the value of low-skill jobs is declining, so that the salaries earned by these workers are falling sharply. Steady work at reasonable wages is becoming impossible for many to find. Unprecedented levels of unemployment and underemployment are predicted as a result of this new postindustrial age. All these developments cast doubt on the familiar belief that anyone willing to work will be able to provide for his or her family.

Naturally, not everyone agrees on the scope and size of the problem, but the growing challenge of a postindustrial economy will surely require us to rethink traditional patterns of organizing our work and time. This is where Catholic social teaching may make an important contribution in the years ahead. The questions raised by these new economic forces are not merely technical matters that might be decided by economists and policymakers alone. Rather, many of the questions about adapting to postindustrialism are above all moral problems on which the Church has much to say. Will our society simply accept a situation in which the highly educated grow ever more fabulously affluent while the less advantaged find themselves further and further cut off from the social mainstream? Do the people who benefit the most from advanced technology owe anything to those unfortunate enough to be born in a region or social class where computers and technological expertise are not easily available? Is it fair to ask a few elites to make adjustments and even serious sacrifices for the benefit of other members of society?

As we have seen, Catholic social teaching does not offer ready-made solutions to any of these questions. But even though its ultimate conclusions and policy preferences might not be immediately obvious, the Church does bring a rich set of resources that help us address these questions. For example, the messages we have seen above about human dignity, solidarity, and the common good suggest that Catholic social teaching would generally support measures that protect the weakest members of society from the dangers that accompany a postindustrial order. None of God's children deserves to be considered merely as a "surplus person." Even those who are unlucky enough to possess few marketable skills cannot simply be ignored and tossed aside by the winners in economic competition. The material needs of all people make a serious claim on all members of the human family, and the artificial boundaries of political allegiance, class, and race will never be an acceptable excuse for continued indifference to our neighbors.

These are a few of the ideas that might form the outline for a future church approach to the challenge of a postindustrial economy. They stretch the message of previous

Catholic social teaching so that it covers a new set of problems in our increasingly globalized context. These suggestions extend the arguments that have been cited in support of the "preferential option for the poor" so that they now address the needs of a new group of people whose prospects are being threatened by the economic forces of our computer age. It may well be that the Church's message on these issues will be ignored until some massive dislocation, such as a refugee crisis, famine, or massive outbreak of unemployment caused by financial collapse, prompts a desperate search for wisdom about the morality of letting people starve. But we can still hope for a more agreeable outcome, where a gradual sharing of the insights of Catholic social teaching helps shape a worldwide reform of institutions that learn to reflect the message of justice and social responsibility for all our neighbors.

The Surprising Future

This chapter has attempted to peek into the future and predict some of the concerns that are likely to find their way into future documents of Catholic social teaching. These guesses may prove to be mistaken, and new items not foreseen in these pages may turn out to be more important. The only thing that would be completely surprising is if God ceased to send us new surprises!

It might be appropriate to close this book with a reminder that places the contribution of Catholic social teaching in proper perspective. Even if popes and bishops suddenly decided to stop writing encyclicals and publishing documents on social issues, the work of the Church in pursuing justice would not cease. The God of justice is present wherever Christian people, motivated by their faith and acting on convictions about the proper ordering of political and economic life in society, engage in efforts to make the world a place of greater fairness and peace. Just as no one may limit the actions of the Holy Spirit, it is impossible to chain the gospel of peace and justice.

What we often need most is not another bishops' committee or another encyclical to quote but, rather, a greater commitment on the part of many of the faithful to live out their beliefs about social justice in a courageous yet prudent way. In order for this to happen, the Church will require people of many talents to apply their efforts in advancing the social mission of the Church. Those who participate will learn to work together like the parts of a body. Some will play the role of the "tongue," teaching and preaching about the themes of Catholic social teaching. Others will be the "hands" of this faith-based justice, lifted up to God in prayer

or thrust down into the earth, grinding soil under the finger-
nails as our collective social involvement grows deeper.
Others may be the "eyes," gathering new information about
our fragile world and contributing to projects of social analysis that will illuminate the footsteps of all on the paths of justice. Catholic social teaching will only be as effective as those
of us who put it into action.

Chapter one began with three brief stories of ordinary
people faced with decisions about how to live out justice in
some small way. It might be helpful to look back at those
three scenarios and take stock of the journey we have traveled.
The praiseworthy choices made in each of those stories may
be understood merely as momentary and isolated acts of generosity. But they may also be seen as important signs of a life-
long commitment to the pursuit of justice, a commitment
that responds to God's call to all of us to practice social
responsibility. Like the people in these stories, those of us
who seek to make a real difference in the world may easily be
overwhelmed by the many choices we face when we look at
human society, with all the complexities of competing political and economic systems. Each one of us may be reassured
that we are not alone and need not "reinvent the wheel" as we
discern our personal calling. Instead, we are already, in a
sense, standing on the shoulders of giants. Catholic social
teaching offers us an extremely helpful tradition of thought

about why and how to practice justice and follow the call of Jesus to "come and see."

Questions for Reflection

1. Does the concept of personalism add anything new to Catholic social teaching? In what ways is it a helpful word to use when we think about social justice?

2. As you think about your daily activities, how helpful do you find the concept of "social sin" as it appears in recent Catholic theology? What benefits do we derive from thinking about our participation in large social structures as sometimes having a sinful dimension? Or is this a misleading idea?

3. Can you relate any significant experiences of the ways, positive or negative, women have been treated within the Church? What changes in church structures, procedures, and opportunities would you suggest to achieve greater gender justice?

4. What suggestions would you offer for improving the process by which encyclicals are written? How can wider participation be encouraged without sacrificing

the unity and integrity of the documents of Catholic social teaching?

5. Do you think that concern for the health of the natural environment is mostly consistent with previous Catholic social teaching, or do ecological priorities generally conflict with this worldview that places humans at the center of creation? How can we resolve the tensions and trade-offs?

6. Do you agree that we are indeed entering a new era as described by the prophets of postindustrialism? If so, how will the Church be challenged to respond to the realities of this new era?

For Further Study

Chapter 1

Day, Dorothy. *The Long Loneliness: An Autobiography*. New York: Harper and Row Publishers, Inc, 1952.

Henriot, Peter J., Edward P. DeBerri and Michael J. Schultheiss. *Catholic Social Teaching: Our Best Kept Secret*. Maryknoll, NY: Orbis Books, 1985.

O'Neill, Michael. "Religion: Godmother of the Nonprofit Sector" in his *The Third America: The Emergence of the Nonprofit Sector in the United States*. San Francisco: Jossey-Bass Publishers, 1989.

Chapter 2

Abbott, Walter M., ed. *The Documents of Vatican II*. New York: America Press, 1966.

Ahlstrom, Sydney E. *A Religious History of the American People*. New Haven, Connecticut: Yale University Press, 1972.

Chadwick, Owen. *The Early Church*. New York: Viking Penguin Inc., 1967.

Coleman, John A. *An American Strategic Theology*. New York: Paulist Press, 1982.

Niebuhr, H. Richard. *Christ and Culture*. New York: Harper and Row Publishers, Inc., 1951.

St. Augustine of Hippo. *The City of God*. New York: Image Books of Doubleday, 1958.

Chapter 3

Bokenkotter, Thomas. *Church and Revolution: Catholics in the Struggle for Democracy and Social Justice*. New York: Image Books of Doubleday, 1998.

Coleman, John A., ed. *One Hundred Years of Catholic Social Thought: Celebration and Challenge*. Maryknoll, NY: Orbis Books, 1991.

Curran, Charles E. and Richard A. McCormick, S.J. *Readings in Moral Theology No. 5: Official Catholic Social Teaching*. New York: Paulist Press, 1986.

Dorr, Donal. *Option for the Poor: A Hundred Years of Vatican Social Teaching*. Maryknoll, NY: Orbis Books, 1992.
–Note: This volume contains detailed treatments of the contents and contexts of all the major social encyclicals.

Hrier Mich, Marvin L. *Catholic Social Teaching and Movements*. Mystic, CT: Twenty-Third Publications, 1998.

Land, Philip S. *Catholic Social Teaching: As I Have Lived, Loathed and Loved It*. Chicago: Loyola University Press, 1994.

O'Brien, David J. and Thomas A. Shannon, eds. *Catholic Social Teaching: The Documentary Heritage*. Maryknoll, NY: Orbis Books, 1992.
–Note: This volume contains the English translations of all twelve texts listed in Table 1, as well as the U.S. bishops' pastoral letters "The Challenge of Peace" and "Economic Justice for All."

Chapter 4

Coleman, John A. and T. Howland Sanks, eds. *Reading the Signs of the Times: Resources for Social and Cultural Analysis*. New York: Paulist Press, 1993.

Curran, Charles E. and Richard A. McCormick, S.J., eds. *Readings in Moral Theology No. 7: Natural Law and Theology*. New York: Paulist Press, 1991.

Haughey, John C., ed. *The Faith that Does Justice: Examining the Christian Sources for Social Change*. New York: Paulist Press, 1977.

Holland, Joe and Peter Henriot. *Social Analysis: Linking Faith and Justice*. Maryknoll, NY: Orbis Books, 1983.

Phan, Peter C., ed. *Social Thought: Messages of the Fathers of the Church*. Wilmington, DE: Michael Glazier, Inc.,1984.

Chapter 5

Bernardin, Joseph Cardinal. *Consistent Ethic of Life*. Thomas G. Fuechtmann, ed. Kansas City, MO: Sheed & Ward, 1988.

Byron, William J. "Ten Building Blocks of Catholic Social Teaching." *America*, 31 October 1998, pp. 9–12.

Fahey, Joseph J. and Richard Armstrong, eds. *A Peace Reader: Essential Readings on War, Justice, Non-violence and World Order*. New York: Paulist Press, 1992.

National Conference of Catholic Bishops. "Sharing Catholic Social Teaching: Challenges and Directions—Reflections of the U.S. Catholic Bishops." Washington, D.C.: United States Catholic Conference, 1998.

O'Brien, David J. and Thomas A. Shannon, eds. *Catholic Social Thought: The Documentary Heritage*. New York: Paulist Press, 1992.

–Note: This volume contains the full texts of all the social teaching documents discussed in this chapter.

Vatican Congregation for Catholic Education. "Guidelines for the Study and Teaching of the Church's Social Doctrine in the Formation of Priests." *Origins* 19, no. 11 (3 August 1989), pp. 169, 171–91.

Chapter 6

Cort, John C. *Christian Socialism: An Informal History.* Maryknoll, NY: Orbis Books, 1988.

Hobgood, Mary E. *Catholic Social Teaching and Economic Theory.* Philadelphia: Temple University Press, 1991.

Massaro, Thomas. *Catholic Social Teaching and United States Welfare Reform.* Collegeville, MN: Liturgical Press, 1998.

Novak, Michael. *Freedom with Justice: Catholic Social Thought and Liberal Institutions.* San Francisco: Harper and Row Publishers, Inc., 1984.

Chapter 7

Christiansen, Drew and Walter Grazer, eds. *"And God Saw That It Was Good": Catholic Theology and the Environment.* Washington, D.C.: United States Catholic Conference, 1996.

Dwyer, Judith A., ed. *The New Dictionary of Catholic Social Thought.* Collegeville, MN: The Liturgical Press, 1994.

Kammer, Fred. *Doing Faithjustice: An Introduction to Catholic Social Thought.* New York: Paulist Press, 1991.

Kammer, Fred. *Salted With Fire: Spirituality for the Faithjustice Journey.* New York: Paulist Press, 1995.

Osiek, Carolyn. *Beyond Anger: On Being a Feminist in the Church.* New York: Paulist Press, 1986.

Rifkin, Jeremy. *The End of Work: The Decline of the Global Labor Force and the Dawn of the Post-Market Era.* New York: G. P. Putnam's Sons, 1995.

Index